WINTER IN ENGLAND

WINTER
IN ENGLAND

by

Nicholas Wollaston

READERS UNION
HODDER AND STOUGHTON
London 1966

This RU edition was produced in 1966 for sale to its members only by Readers Union Ltd, at Aldine House, 10-13 Bedford Street, London W.C.2 and at Letchworth Garden City, Herts. Full details of membership may be obtained from our London address. The book is set in 11 point Garamond type leaded and has been reprinted by Ebenezer Baylis & Son Ltd, Worcester. It was first published by Hodder and Stoughton Ltd.

PROLOGUE

WINTER in England is not the common season for travelling, but though I spun my winter out from late summer to early spring and confined my England to a dozen or so unfashionable places up and down the country, I made only a common journey. It was neither luxurious nor exacting, it led neither to a destination nor to any conclusions, its progress was erratic, its theme spasmodic, and its object only curiosity. But if it was uneventful and even inarticulate, it was not monotonous. I chose my places both for being eccentric and for being typical, for their secrets as well as for their characteristics; and I visited them in a sequence in which, like the courses of a feast, I hoped each would derive some extra piquancy from the last, and would in its turn contribute something to the flavour of the next.

As with all great feasts, at the end I had no special feelings except one of indulgence. I had enjoyed it, I knew, but dyspepsia benumbed my appreciation, and I could no more have said which episode was the most stimulating or the most nourishing, or even which gave me most pleasure, than I could have gone back to Butlin's and begun all over again. For this reason I am afraid that to anybody else it may seem that sometimes my appetite did no justice to the dish before me, and that I merely smothered it with the condiments of my own prejudice and swallowed it as best I could. I can only hope that the total effect is not entirely one of ingratitude to those men and women of England who were my hosts. And to those—especially the vicar of Ockbrook, and Tom the painter of Sutton Hollow, and Michael of Newmarket who took me coursing, and Jumbo Fiske of Lowestoft, and Harry and his friends in the clubs at Blyth, and the kind lady who invited me to the grouse moor above Ramsgill, and the friars of Cerne Abbas, and the mayors and town clerks and factory managers and publicans and strangers wherever I went—to those who generously gave me their hospitality and assistance, and who in return got scarcely a passing nod, I would offer my apologies and gratefulness.

The winter was that of 1963–4, so far from being one of discontent in England as to be one of a satisfaction that bordered almost on complacence. It was the first winter after the coldest one for a century or two; it was the winter when a fourteenth earl became Prime Minister, and when, to seal the memories of a scandalous summer, Christine Keeler was sent to prison; it was the winter when a tunnel under the River Thames was opened, a hundred and sixty-four years after the decision had been taken to build it, and the winter when a decision was taken to build a tunnel under the English Channel; it was the winter of half a million unemployed, and of four new royal babies; it was the winter of the Beatles.

But to me these were not significant. The previous winter I had been to British Guiana; in other recent winters I had travelled in Cuba, across China, over the Sahara, down the river Mekong of Indo-China, through the republics of Central America, among the villages of India and Persia and the islands of the Caribbean and the Pacific Ocean. This winter I chose the temples and jungles of England, as obscure and murky as the rest, but more exciting and more sinister for being my own.

CONTENTS

	PROLOGUE	*page* 5
I	SKEGNESS	11
II	RAMSGILL	19
III	BLYTH	32
IV	LEEK	49
V	LUDLOW	59
VI	BRIDGWATER	66
VII	SWANAGE	78
VIII	LOWESTOFT	85
IX	LIVERPOOL	98
X	SUTTON HOLLOW	111
XI	CORBY	116
XII	WISBECH	130
XIII	CHERTSEY	139
XIV	OCKBROOK	149
XV	NEWMARKET	161
XVI	CERNE ABBAS	173
XVII	BURNLEY	185

ILLUSTRATIONS

between pages 96 and 97

SKEGNESS TWISTERS

SKEGNESS MIDDLE-AGED

LEEK PIN-UP

BRIDGWATER SCEPTICS

LIVERPOOL DOCK

LIVERPOOL CAVERN CLUB

LIVERPOOL SUNSET

CORBY ORE TRAIN

CHERTSEY COMMUTERS

NEWMARKET SPECTATORS

BURNLEY POLICEMAN

1*

SKEGNESS

THE Skegness Holiday Camp Special pulled out of King's Cross station into the August drizzle, half empty, dirty, and fifteen minutes late. On the platform two efficient girls in Butlin's uniform—red blazers and white skirts—directed campers into the carriage reserved for them. They were the Redcoats, the cheerful people employed by Butlin's to put the 'jolly' into my holiday. Terrified, I dodged past them and settled in a compartment at the other end of the train.

Through the grubby windows East Anglia was particularly miserable, the towns buttoning themselves up against a wet Bank Holiday, the wheat and barley flattened by the weather. At level crossings family saloons waited patiently in dozens, their windscreen wipers switched off and the rain bouncing on their two-tone paintwork. The brick kilns of Peterborough looked warm, and I began to wish I was getting out; at Boston I very nearly did. For miles, as the train drove on over brown canals, past solemn rows of poplars, through a meadow with forlorn thistles and a horse, across endless fields of future potato chips, I clung to the fading blur of Boston Stump across the fens.

At Skegness station there were more Redcoats, men this time, in blazers and white flannels, waiting for us. They headed us off from the public exit and into a special yard where we were put into buses, like refugees with a disease. Ten minutes later we were put out at the Reception Block; now we were prisoners. Welcome to Butlin's! You're about to have the holiday of your lives.

I paid fifteen pounds for a week's stay, seven super jollidays, and was given the key to my chalet; with relief I discovered that I was not going to share it with anybody else.

"I know it's an expensive holiday," said an elderly Yorkshire woman that evening, who was an experienced camper, "but there's no fuss. It's all done for you. All you've to do is walk from one place to another and Bob's your uncle." Then she laughed as if she had thought of it for the first time: "Actually, Bob's my husband", and she nudged him. Like a battered old parrot he rubbed his jaw on his shoulder and said that Butlin's was fine, much better than going to a boarding-house or a hotel and having to pay for all your entertainment. "And it's all on the flat, for walking, and with my complaint I can't go up and down."

"Bob's had a cerebral," said his wife.

Certainly there was a great deal of walking, even in the rain. The nine thousand of my fellow-campers seemed to be always strolling or bustling along the camp's main street, apparently looking for something that I suspect they didn't even know they could never find. Gangs of teen-age boys rushed excitedly from one end of the camp to the other, shouting. A lost child went sobbing through the crowd, while people stood aside and said, "Oh, poor kid, it's lost." Elsewhere they might have done something, but at Butlin's responsibility was not their business; there was bound to be a special Redcoat for the job, anyway.

Huge painted clowns and toy soldiers were fixed to the concrete buildings, and the trees were linked by strings of coloured lights hanging in plastic kitchen colanders. The big baubles dangling in the rain looked faintly familiar, which bothered me for a few days until I thought I recognized the Oxford Street decorations from a recent Christmas, a little soiled after their London season but still good enough for a few summers on the coast of Lincolnshire. They had brought something of the flavour of Oxford Street with them.

In the covered Viennese Beer Garden a sham water-wheel splashed weakly in a cement trough, and dusty cockatoos swung from the ceiling. In Ye Olde Pig and Whistle hundreds of cards with funny jokes written on them twisted slowly on strings — jokes about mothers-in-law and honeymoons and dirty old men. In the Tudor Bar elderly campers yawned under a gigantic plaster tree, or giggled at the plight of a real pigeon that had flown in and was battering itself among the saucy little lattice windows above them. Even the indoor swimming-pool lay under a jungle of synthetic greenery. This obsession with the bogus and the dangling may have served to disguise the architecture of the buildings, and certainly the rain that in places dripped through the roof added authenticity to the picturesque settings, but it was disappointing to find that so few modern ideas of design had been adopted. The Festival of Britain might never have happened.

"It's what the campers like," a Redcoat told me, and that is a sad thing.

That first day the pattern of a Butlin's jolliday emerged. During the long hours between bar opening times the big public rooms were like the waiting-room of a railway terminus, full of people waiting for a train to take them on a holiday—except that now they were all waiting for it to take them home again. The rain, of course, deprived them of much of the fun they had come for, but at almost any time of the day or evening there was one consolation that made up even for the weather: bingo.

Bingo abounded, an infestation. From every other doorway came the ritual sound: "Four and eight, forty-eight. Two little ducks, twenty-two." The amusement arcades were crammed with young men pumping money into the machines, the one-armed bandits swallowing coins as though possessed by insatiable, money-eating tapeworms, and being kicked for not coughing up the promised prizes; but nothing was as popular as bingo. It droned on in every cafeteria, the coy formula and the barren, thrill-less waste; its votaries seemed quite numbed by the monotony, ticking off the numbers and scarcely smiling even when they won a prize, but reaching for another sixpence and settling down again. Some of them kept their transistor radios beside them, switched on all the time. "Kelly's eye, number one. All the fours, forty-four."

Two clergymen appeared for a moment at the door of a pin-table saloon and watched the players, rather embarrassed, rather shocked, and perhaps rather wishing to join in. A girl in jeans and curlers pumped a fruit-machine, one hand in the pocket of a boy in jeans and ringlets. The bingo caller—for there was bingo going on even in the saloons—saw me idling by the machines and squawked into the microphone, "Come along, campers, don't be shy, there's a seat at the end there, any line for a win, top to bottom, side to side, corner to corner, sixpence a time, heads down for the next house, all the sixes, clickety-click."

I slipped away and went for a drink in the Empress Bar, near a man with a cigarette holder and a pint of beer sitting with a girl with ivory hair, blue eyelids and a Babycham.

He said, "They might have served the pudding up for soup, for all the difference there was."

She said, "Stephen Ward dying like that—do you think it'll make any difference to Christine Keeler?"

Later, I went to a variety show in the theatre. Every performer, however bad, was received with whistling and clapping. A comedian made a joke about a coloured woman, and I suddenly realised that I hadn't seen a black camper yet; nor did I until my last morning, when I saw a white woman with two half-caste children. A young couple came into the theatre late, and the comedian sized them up straight away: "Honeymooners! Give them a big hand, campers, a very big hand." And to shrieks from the audience he followed it up with a couple of gags pinched from the naughty postcards in the camp newspaper shop. I couldn't see how the honeymooners were taking it, and I tried to guess.

Later still, I went back to Ye Olde Pig and Whistle, now a vast den of noise and beer, with all those funny jokes hanging in the smoke overhead. The boys shouted and clapped, and the beer swilled deeper, while a brave and beautiful woman with a club foot sang into a microphone. Her voice bellowed from loud-speakers hidden behind the jokes, it set up sympathetic noises in the youths and in the imitation woodwork, and sent waves rippling through the beer; it was a magnificent voice, a baritone.

I ended up that night with most of my fellow nine thousand campers in the fish and chip shop in the middle of the camp, the ultimate shrine where there wasn't any bingo, but only fish, chips, bread and butter and tea for three-and-sixpence. I said I didn't want the tea.

"You've got to pay for it, so you'd better have it," said the woman fiercely.

I sat at a table with three young men who had come down from Dundee. The sun had been shining in Scotland that morning, they said sadly, looking out at the drizzle, and they had expected to find it even hotter in England. But at least it was exciting. The speed of everything was what impressed them most, and the activity. English people seemed to be always rushing about. And in the Butlin's bars they didn't just sit in silence and drink, as they did in pubs in Scotland, but were for ever talking and laughing and singing, or jumping up to the stage to take the microphone. The Rock 'n' Twist Ballroom terrified them most of all: all those teen-agers sweating with energy, and not even drinking beer.

*　　　*　　　*

At seven-thirty on Bank Holiday morning a voice rolled over the chalets: "Good morning, campers! It's raining again today" — (making it sound almost a thrill) — "but remember, it's always fun at Butlin's."

My damp little chalet and the cracked cement round the wash-basin were only too familiar, dragging up memories that I half hoped were lost. For I had been in that camp once before, nineteen years earlier.

During the war it was commandeered by the navy and became one of His Majesty's ships, with an officer of the watch, a quarter deck, and liberty boats down the road to Skegness. It was there that I joined up as an ordinary seaman and was given a six-figure number and three shillings a day. It had been a fortnight of inoculations, kit issues, lectures on tooth decay, and squad drill under a gunner who prided himself on being the only petty officer in the navy ever to hold a certificate of mental deficiency, and under whose hideous eye I learnt how to lash a hammock, to fold my bell-bottom trousers, and to tie a sheepshank.

This time it all came back: the bleak view through barbed wire of the beach and a hazy convoy of ships in the North Sea, the terror of making a mistake and being marched by the mad gunner before the officer of the watch, and the agony of sickness after too much beer in the canteen. Even my six-figure number came back, and things that I hadn't cared to think of for nineteen years, like the special lavatories with V.D. painted on the door, and my shock one evening when another public schoolboy, going into Skegness by the same liberty boat as myself, slipped into the sick-bay for his free ration of contraceptives. That was more than half my life ago.

I had expected the same kind of regimentation again, but it was almost worse at Butlin's: a discreet, patronising authority instead of an exhausting discipline, less beastly, more disheartening, and ineffably demoralising. That nine thousand holiday-makers appeared to be enjoying it only showed how bleak their other lives must have been; though sometimes, at the sight of the women hurrying from one bingo hall to another and of the men standing outside the betting shop feebly whistling the tune of the nearest transistor radio, I wondered how happy they were. Butlin's told them loudly that they were having fun, and they believed it. If they had stopped to think, they might have begun to wonder, but the whole point of Butlin's was that it was a holiday from thinking. They could have had no delusions about escaping from anything else, if that had ever been their idea, for at the other end of the loudspeakers there was always somebody to remind them, at the slightest hint of submission, that the whole multi-million entertainment machine would gladly scoop them up. Butlin's may once have been only a fairground side-show with a knack of drawing customers by its proprietor's personality, but the little hoop-la stall had now become a factory, a tycoon's process for manufacturing jollidays, and the showman's patter had been drowned by the eager whoops of his Redcoats.

Fears of regimentation were deliberately assuaged by an official policy of do-as-you-please and a soothing use of the second person: your breakfast is now ready for you; your Redcoats will be happy to help you; here is your entertainment programme for this afternoon. But in case anybody should have unsociable ideas about holiday behaviour, there was always a stern voice to correct them. Outside Ye Olde Pig and Whistle at night a squad of commissionaires in blue and yellow uniform glowered at the young men coming out. And at lunch one day, after the rallying cry of a Redcoat had stirred us to a cheer, the loudspeakers called for silence while the camp controller came on the air; in a severe voice he announced that he had just sent twelve campers home for making trouble in the chalet lines the night before: "Campers, I can assure you that I won't hesitate to do the same again. For nobody is going to spoil your holiday at Butlin's, which you have all done so much to earn."

I wondered what the mad gunner was doing nowadays.

*   *   *

If a week of jollidays was the paroxysm of revelry which Butlin's tried to make it, it was also a feast for the advertisers. The competitions for the bathing beauty, the mother and child, the glamorous grandmother, the bonny baby, old-time dancing, and the girl with the best dress sense were all sponsored by various newspapers; darts, toy car racing, the family group, and the girl with the best complexion were sponsored by different brands of soup, beer, soap and cigarettes. Only the contests for Mister Knobbly Knees (for lads over sixteen) and Miss Chubby (for lasses up to fifty) had no commercial godmother.

I had never before watched a beauty competition, and I vaguely expected to find it beautiful, funny, or even, with luck, lascivious. But like so much else at Butlin's it turned out to be just absurdly boring. I didn't even pick the winner.

About fifty girls, fully dressed, lined up in the Prince's Ballroom, some of them as plain as possible and others very pretty indeed. Three-quarters of them were quickly weeded out, and the finalists strutted back in bathing-suits and high-heeled shoes. A compère delivered a commentary, cracking the same jokes that he had made every week of the season, and Redcoat men fooled around with the competitors. Each girl stood alone for a minute on a platform, then turned round to show the other side, while the judges solemnly noted down her points and a camera flashed. A cuddly piece in a bikini was tickled all over by a Redcoat with an ostrich feather, to shrieks from the audience; she nearly burst into tears. The girl I fancied didn't even win a place, and the judges gave first prize to an inaccessible-looking professional who knew how to bend one knee and put on a rigid smile, but who was as synthetic as glamour could make her; she was clearly heading for the finals at the Albert Hall. The camera flashed harder than ever, while the judges fixed a purple sash across her bathing-suit and the compère made an attempt to kiss her plastic cheek.

Far more memorable, because it was so ignominious, was the trial for Mister Knobbly Knees. I cowered at the back of the crowd, horribly conscious of my own potential, while Redcoats hauled promising candidates into the paddock. They were then lined up in batches and ordered to pull up their trousers and display their knees. As if that were not humiliating enough, the compère made them bend and kick, while the audience howled with laughter — the awful laughter of a thousand people infinitely happy that it wasn't their own ordeal. One victim in the line was singled out for special degradation and put through a grotesque solo of his own, in front of the others; his agony was almost worse because he managed to endure it cheerfully. Anyway, who were Butlin's, I wondered, to profit from the knobbles on a poor man's knees?

When the rain stopped I went through the gate in the camp fence and on to the beach. Here was another world, another English way of making holidays: family cricket on the wet sand, dads with rolled-up trousers digging sand castles for their sons, mums screaming at their daughters, daughters screaming at themselves, old men staring out to sea. One stout gent asleep in a deckchair had his pipe stuck into his fly-buttons. A man walked down the beach selling cockles in a basket. Another man in a green tweed jacket, with a green tweed shirt and a green tweed tie, gave me a suggestive look as he passed; it could never have happened in Butlin's.

"Do you take photos, mister?" a woman shouted at me. When I said No, she said, "I only wanted to know." Then she smiled, and added, "I didn't think so."

There wasn't a Redcoat in sight, or a loudspeaker, and the transistor radios were all on different stations. The loudest noise came from a missionary with a megaphone, trying to amuse a crowd of children. A damp bevy of donkeys was tethered to a breakwater; on the sea was a single blue sail, and in the sky were kites and a funny, spluttering old aeroplane.

On my way back into Butlin's I noticed the withering slogan painted on a merry-go-round in the camp fun fair: "Holidays are jollidays on the golden gallopers, so ride 'em, campers, at the sticks. Tally-ho!" Suddenly the sea was far away.

II

RAMSGILL

A KNICKERBOCKERED bird-watcher sweeping the Bradford city reservoir through field-glasses, a young man crouching over his trout rod to tie on another fly, an old-fashioned hiker stalking up the valley in long khaki shorts with a pink hairless head and a snort of scorn for each car that passed on its way to the local beauty spot, Yorkshire's Little Switzerland — these were the nearest things in sight to a Butlin's camper. It was pleasantly impossible to remember what it had been like at Skegness and though, for all I knew, the evening sun was shining there too, it could never have been doing it so prettily as in the ash-trees and sycamores of Nidderdale.

In the purple-grey village of Lofthouse, a stone huddle overlooking the valley bottom, a bull glared at me across a wall and yellow horseflies flew up from the cowpats in the steep little street. For a moment, at the sight of a tell-tale paper stuck to a barn door, I thought I heard the bingo huckster calling, but it was only a hand-written notice to say there would be a dance one night — next month, last month, some time — to the Dixielanders. A purist might find gloom in the chipped orange plaque advertising Brooke Bond Dividend Tea, though nobody could complain at the inscription on the war memorial pump: "If you want to be healthy, wealthy and stout, use plenty of cold water inside and out." Not even the mottoes swinging from the ceiling of Ye Olde Pig and Whistle could achieve such exquisite vacuity. "Let animal and man drink freely," it added, for emphasis.

Animal and man may not still drink side by side in Lofthouse, but to an outsider the village has that feeling — a disturbing, atavistic feeling, as if the people and their cows and sheep share an ancient and almost holy secret — which one sometimes senses in the poorest parts of Italy or Spain, but which must be rare in England now. Not that the farmers of Nidderdale are badly off; from milk, wool and lambs, or from fattening Irish cattle to sell down on the plain of York, they make a fair living, even if at some season most of them may have to borrow money from the bank at Pateley Bridge. But the bank manager himself, who came to the dale from Leeds, told me that it took him several years to realise just how old were the ways of the Nidderdale farmers.

The more prosperous they become, the sooner will that ancient feeling disappear, and already there are signs that Nidderdale is going the way of all England. In Lofthouse one cottage with its windows freshly painted and a name on the door, 'Stoneywalls', had a new garage beside it, to mark it from the anonymous house next door which only had a motorbike and sidecar. Down at Ramsgill, at the head of the reservoir, every other cottage had been bought or rented by weekenders from the cities, at prices that reflected no lack of modern ideas among the villagers. And in Pateley Bridge two small groceries were empty and shuttered up; with more money and better transport many people prefer now to go down to Harrogate for a weekly shopping trip and a bit of fun. Only the little old mills down by the river, making rope and twine, seem to be oblivious of these fashions, and the bank manager said he thought it was because they had missed their chance years ago and now it was too late. Their huge water-wheels splash and creak as they have done for centuries, twisting the good hemp as if coal and oil and nylon were words of the devil; and in a hard winter they still get frozen up for months on end.

The Yorke Arms at Ramsgill, like other pubs in Nidderdale, has fallen to outsiders, not even to Yorkshiremen, and its character must have changed with the invasion. It is probably less of a pub, more of a hotel, than it used to be, with more copper and brass about the place, and a breathtaking upper-class waitress on holiday from a domestic science college, who can laugh off the ladders in her stockings as ingenuously as she explains that the bilberries in the tart are frozen, actually. Though some of the beer in the bar is still kept in wooden barrels, most of it comes from steel casks or bottles, and I suppose that the customers are not quite what they used to be, either.

"Now let me see, where were you at school?" said a man to me in the bar my first evening, and I tried to remember when I had last been asked; I saw that it was important.

But he was an agreeable man, and I drank a lot of beer with him, mostly at his expense. A week or two earlier he had been down to London on business and had taken his daughter out in the evening. "She's eighteen. Got a flat there and learning to be a secretary; you know, like all the others. I took her to dinner at the Hilton. We were finished by half past eight, and honestly, I didn't know what to do with her. Didn't know what to say to her, though she's my own daughter. I couldn't face an evening like that, so we went to the cinema. Hadn't been to the cinema for years. We went to this wide screen thing; you know, Cinerama, where everything comes at you from all sides. Bloody marvellous. Honestly, I hadn't taken out a girl of eighteen for about a hundred years. She enjoyed it, though. I just didn't know what to say to her. Now let me see" — he turned to a stranger at the bar — "that tie you're wearing; it's the Fourteenth-Twentieth, if I'm not much mistaken."

"Good God, no," replied the other man. "It's the Alwoodley Golf Club. You know, on the road to Leeds."

I liked the company in the Yorke Arms, and I liked the company one evening in a little field high above Ramsgill at the edge of the moors, where the Harker brothers were bringing in the last of their hay. They were the third generation to be born in that windy, moorside farmhouse, and the little girl driving the tractor belonged to the fourth. The year before, their farm had been connected to the telephone and the electricity supply, though the new wooden hay-rakes leaning against the stone wall of the field showed that they hadn't quite forsaken the past. The Harkers were in a hurry that evening, and that too was traditional; the hay must be carted, for the next day, the Glorious Twelfth of August, they would all be out beating on the grouse moors.

*   *   *

Albert, the gamekeeper at Ramsgill, a raw little man who had been wounded with the Gunners in the First World War and now played the cornet in a local silver band, took me up the valley to Middlesmoor on Sunday afternoon to meet Archie Menzies, another keeper. We went through Archie's kitchen, full of women and babies and a huge dresser bearing the best dinner service, into the front parlour where Archie was asleep with the Sunday paper in front of an electric fire, the grate being already full of cigarette packets and Black Magic chocolate boxes. He wasn't too pleased to see us at first, but Mrs Menzies brought cups of tea on a brass Benares tray and Archie slowly became hospitable.

He had left Perthshire before the last war and spent many years as keeper at Middlesmoor, a neat mountain village perched at the head of the watery dale where the flat-topped moors fold over on to the little walled fields. He almost admitted that the view from his house down to the pink willow herb and the reservoir in the distance was as good as anything in Scotland.

But a keeper's life was nothing to what it had been. As a young man, Archie had been one of fourteen keepers on a big highland estate where now they only kept two. The shooting, as on so many estates, had been bought by a syndicate, and although there was a captain of the syndicate he wasn't the same as the old laird. In those days the estate had been a complete social community, where service had also meant self-respect, and where, even if wages were low, there had been compensations; the second butler, for instance, had always been ready to open up a bottle of his master's whisky, and as well as fourteen keepers there had been fourteen housemaids, who had come in handy on winter nights after the grouse-shooting season. Nowadays their place had been taken by electric washing-machines, and what could you do with a washing-machine?

Archie the Scot and Albert the Yorkshireman, in their rough tweed knickerbocker suits and in their rough, dry sentences, lamented the old life of a gamekeeper. They lamented, too, the old life of the dale villages. The pub had long since ceased to be the men's meeting place; what with all this gassy tankard beer and all these weekenders the villagers preferred to take a few bottles home and watch the television, though even that had begun to lose its attraction.

"I don't know when I last saw it, do you, Albert?"

There were no village concerts these days, and in a place where everyone had once known what everyone else was up to, now nobody seemed to care. There had been a time when twenty people would cycle together down to the cinema in Pateley Bridge, and after the pubs had shut would cycle seven miles and nearly a thousand feet back again. There had been a time when the owner of a moor would send a couple of eighteen-gallon barrels of beer up by pony for the beaters, and it would all be drunk, but nowadays if they got through a couple of dozen bottles on a hot day it was unusual.

"There's not the call for it, is there, Albert? They seem to prefer tea. I don't know what's happened."

"Mind you, I like tea myself," said Albert hastily.

Even the gentlemen had grown soft. Grouse shooting was now all done by driving the birds to the butts, never by walking-up over the moors, and to look at the figures of some of the shooters who came to Nidderdale these days it was easy to see why. Archie could remember a squire who made his small son walk with him all day over the moors carrying a crow-bar on his shoulder, to condition him for when he would be allowed to carry a gun.

The two keepers were just as gloomy about the year's prospects for grouse. A bad winter had done surprisingly little damage and there was plenty of heather, the birds' main food, but heavy rain in the early summer had wrought havoc with the chicks, hundreds of which had simply been drowned, and there were not half as many young birds as usual. Archie had advised his own syndicate not to shoot on their moor until September, and because his advice was important in the valley the owners of several of the other moors were going to wait too. In a normal year the opening of the season brought a boost to the local economy, with the shooters spending pots of money in garages, shops and pubs, and paying twenty-five shillings a day to anybody who would enlist as a beater; this year it was different.

But Albert's moor, one of the few private moors not to have sold out to a syndicate, was going to shoot on the Twelfth, though Albert himself thought they would be lucky if they got forty brace of grouse, a third of last year's bag.

*   *   *

We met on the Ramsgill village green after breakfast—nine shooters, a few wives, various keepers, loaders, beaters, dogs, and myself. There was also a photographer from the *Yorkshire Post* who picked out the ladies and gentlemen and lined them up against a Land-Rover. They made a handsome picture, the ladies in tweed and silk, the gentlemen in knickerbocker suits, pressed and pleated and very beautiful. Their servants, in the same splendid clothes but sometimes with canvas puttees round their ankles, were almost indistinguishable, which confused me until I saw that they had slimmer figures and finer, healthier faces. I myself felt very shabby in my old flannel trousers and no hat; I would have given a lot that morning for a pair of brogues or a deer-stalker.

In the middle of the green crouched half a dozen Jaguars, as well turned out as their masters and a little sleeker. We stood among them, admiring their points and talking about engines, ski-ing holidays, girls, business, Jew-boys, and the Socialists. One man had a stone in his kidney, another had a duodenal ulcer, and a third had gone down to London the other day to collect his guns and all he had to do in his E-type on the motorway was set it at a hundred and twenty-five and go to sleep. A young quarry-owner said he had been fishing for blue sharks off Cornwall last week, and he was teased about escaping from the girls down there in time for the grouse shooting.

"Not so good in Cornwall as in Spain, eh my boy?" Two years ago, on the morning of the Twelfth, a telegram had arrived at Ramsgill from him in Madrid to say he couldn't get back in time; it had been a terrible solecism and he hadn't been invited last year, but now he was forgiven. Another man was teased for boasting that he was going to shoot grouse on three more days that week, on different moors: "It's all very well for you; nobody would ever miss you in your office, but there'd be hell to pay if I took as much time off as you do." Somebody told me that whereas in some business firms almost everybody seemed to go in for yachting, in others it was grouse shooting; one or two firms even owned their own grouse moors, which were counted as entertainment expenses for business guests and therefore exempt from taxation. There was much loud laughter in the morning air, while the servants unloaded guns, haversacks and hampers from the Jaguars and stowed them away again in the Land-Rovers.

We crammed ourselves into the Land-Rovers among all the dogs and equipment, and drove up a steep track from the valley to the moor. The gates were opened for us by little farm girls who stood on the bottom bar smiling hopefully.

"Who's got sixpence? Quick, a sixpence." Then, when the child had been paid and we were driving on, "It used to be a penny, d'you remember?" It used to be a long walk, too, up to the moors, or a pony-ride for the older gentlemen, but Land-Rovers have changed all that, and nowadays nobody has to walk very far, except the beaters.

At the edge of the moor, by a line of stone butts, we stopped and unloaded. I was sent to the end butt, with the young quarry-owner and his dog. He gave me a shooting-stick to sit on, tied up the dog, and then made some practice sighting movements with his gun. It looked very promising.

"Let's see, where were you at school? Oh, really? Did you know a fellow there called . . .?" and then we relaxed and waited, enjoying ourselves. Silence fell across the moor. Patches of sun drifted over the heather, a rainstorm hovered beyond the valley we had come from, a few sheep stirred in front of us, a pigeon rose from a hidden gully, a woman's voice came from the next butt fifty yards away. It was very beautiful—a Yorkshire moor on an August morning, only seven days away from the drizzle of Butlin's—and when my surprise at being there diminished I began to hope that nothing was going to happen at all. For a long time, nothing did.

Then the first grouse appeared, six of them flying low over the heather a long way ahead of us, and almost immediately a row of twenty tiny white flags appeared on the skyline about a mile beyond, as the beaters came over the horizon. Ten minutes later a shot sounded from the other end of the butts, and then there was silence again. I thought that Albert's gloomy prophecy was going to look like wild optimism. But soon birds began to appear in several directions.

A pack of grouse—I called them a covey until I was corrected by the quarry-owner—swept up in front of our butt, coming fast with the wind. He swung his gun over the wall, clicked the safety catch, crouched excitedly like a wrestler, swung again, fired, bang! and fired again, bang! There was a pleasant whiff of cordite, and the pack flew on undamaged. A few minutes later it happened again; crouch, swing, bang! bang! and the lucky birds flew on. The dog stood up, and the quarry-owner told it to sit down.

In the next butt a father and son team, with the mother and a golden labrador behind them, were doing better. I saw a grouse tumble into the heather, followed a second later by the bang. The quarry-owner went on shooting and missing, while spent cartridges piled up around us, scarlet and a little obscene, and seven-pence a time.

"We're not exactly covering ourselves with glory," he said, as a single bird came towards us, high and black against the clouds. I longed for him to shoot it down, surprising myself by my own wish to see it killed. Bang! bang! and it flew away behind us.

"I think I legged it. I hate to do that. Its leg was down, did you see?"

The beaters came on towards us, thrashing the heather and bracken with their flags, hooting and whistling louder to flush the remaining grouse and perhaps to impress the shooters. Four birds flew out of a patch of bracken and sailed right down the line of butts in front of the guns. Shots rang from every butt and two birds jerked in the air, tumbled head over heels and fell to the ground. The other two came over our butt — crouch, swing, bang! bang! — and the birds sailed on. The drive was over.

The dogs were sent off to retrieve the dead grouse, hunting and sniffing and showing only a black tail thrashing above the heather until they came out with a bird, sometimes still nervously flapping, in their mouth. A labrador picked up the scent of a wounded grouse that seemed to have scuttled down a trench in a peat hag, and everybody whistled and shouted.

"It's a runner," said a beater.

"Looks like a runner," said a keeper.

"Must be a runner," said a gentleman.

"A runner!" said a lady.

The owner of the moor came down the line to see how the drive had gone; at the last butt the quarry-owner, before going off to look for the bird he thought he had legged, had to admit that he had nothing else to show.

"Hm, that was an awful lot of banging for no birds."

When the grouse had been recovered, the shooters walked a few hundred yards to the next line of butts. The beaters walked a mile or so back to the edge of the moor to start driving again. This time I stood in a butt with the owner, and although it was a difficult drive, with the birds coming suddenly over a rise in front of the guns and no time to watch them approach, he killed a lot. They thumped on to the grass around us, or pitched in their flight and somersaulted into the heather, leaving a cloud of feathers hanging in the air to mark where they died, like the wreckage from a sunken ship.

For the third drive, a long one right down the top of the moor, I joined the beaters. With a languid man called Ronnie I walked to the beginning of the drive where we waited for the signal to begin. Long ago Ronnie had been articled to a solicitor in Darlington, but during the war he had come up to Nidderdale to teach the farmers to work a tractor. There he had married a dalesman's daughter and taken to farming; he hated going back to Darlington now. Most of the other beaters were Nidderdale farmers and villagers recruited by Albert, or schoolboys up from Pateley Bridge, all walking over the moors for twenty-five shillings a day. There was also a parish priest from a Bradford slum, with his daughter in a scarlet ski-jacket.

"He loves it," said Ronnie. "He comes every year for the Twelfth. Preaching and praying all yesterday, and caught the early bus this morning."

The man next in the line called to us to start beating, and we plunged across a gully, jumped a stream, drove over peat hags and through mossy swamps. With a great clatter a grouse flew up from almost between my feet, circled round and made off back the way I had come, into safety. I felt glad, but guilty. Soon the shots started in front of us, and we all yodelled and hollered louder. I tripped in a hole and crashed down, and thought I heard somebody laugh in one of the butts ahead. Then suddenly the line of beaters had reached the line of butts, and it was time for lunch.

Cold mutton, tongue, salad, cheese, bottles of beer—it was all laid out on a table in the shooting-box, a stone house built in a hollow of the moor. The gentlemen and their ladies occupied the big room, the beaters and keepers and loaders filled the small room next door. The parish priest and his daughter sat outside on the moor. In the gentlemen's room, where a pile of peat was stacked in the corner near the fireplace in case we felt cold, the owner of the moor offered us whisky and sherry, and the guests who hadn't been invited to lunch brought out their own hampers.

"There's the new democracy for you," said a gentleman, seeing one of the guests unpack a colossal canteen of hot food for his loader in the next room.

"He gets more lunch than I do," said the guest, laughing. "He gets a pudding too."

Somebody explained to me the point of separating masters and men: "In here we're saying what bloody bad beaters they are, and in there they're saying what bloody bad shots we are. So everybody's happy."

On a beam above the table were engraved the total bags for the Twelfth of previous years, and sitting under it we made guesses for today's figure, and recounted our morning's adventures. With the good food and beer, and with all those convivial gentlemen—some of whom had hung up their jackets and were sitting in their waistcoats, though none of them had walked more than a few hundred yards from one butt to the next—it was all very pleasant. There was a seedy young American in glasses, who said that he came from California but was studying in Paris and that this was the first time he had been on a hunting trip in England; he felt very honoured. (My neighbour whispered, "One of the quietest Yanks I've ever met; it's nice to know they haven't got something twice as big over there.") And there was a genial pale-faced lord, who had once been Minister of Pensions and who cleared his throat for silence before telling a story about an old woman who went into a grocer's for a bottle of port wine. She was offered some at five-and-six a bottle. Said she, "Is it good for the blood?" Said the grocer, "I don't know about that, but it's bloody good for the money." There were hoots of laughter round the table, polite smiles from the ladies, and great guffaws from the lord himself. When the mirth had subsided he repeated the pay-off line in case anybody had missed it "Is it good for the blood?" "I don't know, but it's bloody good for the money." We laughed all over again, and the second time even the American must have got the joke.

The owner's wife gave us apple pie and Wensleydale cheese, and a steel tycoon from Leeds told me confidentially of an old Yorkshire saying: "Apple pie without some cheese is like a kiss without a squeeze." Then the owner gave us all a tot of cherry brandy before we went out for the last two drives of the day.

A tremendous rainstorm was hanging in the sunshine at the end of the valley, so remote that the quarry-owner and I, in our butt, decided that it would pass far away; but instead it came driving down over the moor, and suddenly it was streaming down my neck and soaking my trousers. The gentlemen in their tweed hats and waterproof jackets had no thoughts but for the grouse, now flying dimly on towards the butts, black in the distance but turning dark red as they approached. Bang! bang! two were hit from another butt and crashed down. Bang! the rest flew on behind us, with the rain.

The storm passed and the sun came out in time for the final drive; we simply had to turn round in our butts and face the other way, while the beaters trudged across the moor to drive back the birds that had got through last time; it hardly seemed fair. But the grouse all went down to the other end of the butts and the quarry-owner didn't get a single shot until the beaters had almost reached us. Then, as with the first drive in the morning, a single grouse came over us, flying high and fast. The quarry-owner crouched, swung his gun, fired once, bang! and the bird tossed in the air, rolled over and plummetted into the heather, leaving its little patch of feathers drifting in the sunshine and a cloud of smoke above us in the butt. "Good shot," came over from the next butt, and I almost felt I had done it myself.

The grouse were collected up into sacks and put in a trailer while we squeezed back into the Land-Rovers, the gentlemen still immaculate in their lovely suits and their boots still polished; the beaters disappeared somewhere over the moor, and the little girls came out again to open the gates for us.

Down on the village green there was a great transferring of stuff from Land-Rovers back into Jaguars, a surreptitious slipping of pound notes into Albert's hand, a lot of laughing and thanking and congratulating. The day's bag was seventy-four and a half brace, a better total than anybody had hoped; most of them would be on the menu that evening in London restaurants at four pounds a bird, some of them were due to fly again—to New York—and only a brace or two each were taken home by the shooters.

"Have to wash bloody Jaguar when we get home," I heard a manservant say, but he was not complaining; it had been a good day. Then, with a dribble from their exhausts and a deep rumble from all their litres, the cars slunk off the grass and out of the village.

*   *   *

Alf was another gamekeeper, but quite different from Albert and Archie. I went over the moors into Wharfedale and found him living in a tall Victorian cottage with purple wooden pinnacles on the gables and a tiled cockscomb along the crest of the roof; it stood in the woods near an old stone bridge. He didn't invite me inside, but took me off to see his pheasants.

With a golden labrador and six Jack Russell terriers we walked over the fields to a wood near an overgrown lake; herons stood among the weeds in front of an abandoned boat-house. The dogs started to chase the scent of a hare, but Alf called them back and sternly told them to lie down in the grass while we walked on into the wood; slowly they crept forward after us, guiltily, until he shouted at them to get back. Like the American on the grouse moor I felt privileged to be allowed into the wood to see Alf's pheasants.

At the end of the shooting season, he told me, any hen pheasants still alive were lured or driven into a fenced-in enclosure and pinioned. The cocks flew in over the top of the fence to get at them, and when the hens had laid enough eggs they were released. The eggs were then hatched by broody chickens.

Alf's pheasant chicks had now grown to the size of pullets, and he had just let them out of their cages to run about in the undergrowth and out into the fields, pecking for insects, though they did not yet stray far from their foster-mothers, the old hens in little wooden coops who were caterwauling in stages of apoplexy, cheated of their families. A hurricane lamp swung from a branch above them, to discourage foxes at night.

Sadly Alf picked up the torn bodies of five young pheasants from the grass. They had been killed, not for food, but out of sheer malice, by a cat, and I asked him how he knew. He showed me where the cat had bitten through the back, not in the spot where a fox or a stoat would have struck, and he pointed to a faint pawmark in the soft earth, the tiny but unmistakable print of a cat. Vermin—a kestrel was hovering over the fields—with poachers and the weather were Alf's three troubles.

He walked to a hut under the trees where he kept food for his pheasants, and unlocked the door.

"Let's see," he said quietly, "Mellors had a hut too, didn't he?"

For a moment, in my astonishment, I couldn't think who he was talking about. But with a smile Alf said he hadn't yet found his Connie Chatterley, hadn't even read the book, didn't hold with filth in literature, and anyway preferred writing books to reading them.

Back at his cottage he took me into his little garden where, among the cabbages and sweet peas, was a wooden tar-blacked hutch, perhaps for tools or chickens. Though it was too small to stand up in, it contained an old armchair and a table with a type-writer, an electric fire and a bulb hanging from the roof; the table and the floor were deep in a chaos of quarto sheets of type-script. Looking through the door it seemed impossible for any-body to get inside; but Alf had written many articles in it, and a play, and he had just finished a book about the life of a game-keeper; now he was going to turn the play into a novel. He reached in and picked out two sheets of paper, the last pages of the book; in passionate, unrestrained language, too full of words to be coherent, they described a girl walking through the woods, and kingfishers flashing over a stream, and an old fox scratching his ear under an oak tree, and memories of Alf's grandfather and his own hopes of achieving the same contentment in his old age.

"It's good, isn't it? I like that ending," he said when I had finished reading. I was too embarrassed to know what to say, but I saw that he was pleased with it, in the way that anybody is pleased who knows he has done something well, and he didn't want to hear my opinion. He didn't really want to talk at all about his writing, and he was glad that nobody in the district knew the secret of his little hutch. His job was gamekeeping, as his father's and grandfather's and great-grandfather's had been, though his own son had gone into market-gardening; he pre-ferred to talk about the countryside, and on this he shared the feelings of Albert and Archie. Shooting syndicates were not like squires, and country life was becoming degenerate with the break-ing up of stately homes and the passing of religion; these week-enders who were buying up the cottages had not a scrap of feeling for the country, and most of them didn't know a pheasant from a sparrow hawk. Alf looked at me critically: "Yourself, would you really like to live in the country?" I had a suspicion that he didn't approve of me, anyway.

III

BLYTH

IT WOULD be too much to expect a coal town on a rainy evening to be a cheerful place, but Blyth must be one of the ugliest towns in England even on a sunny day. It seems to have been turned inside out; its collieries, its shipyard, its port, its power station, its new factories—all the features that justify its existence, indeed its importance—lie on the periphery, and in the middle I could find only a bus station and a bingo hall. Around them spread desolation: derelict houses with boarded-up doors and broken windows, vacant lots littered with saucepans and newspapers, and a vast Methodist church for sale. I nearly went away again, to Wallsend, Jarrow, Sunderland—they all sounded bad, but none of them could be worse than Blyth.

Although it was still August coal fires had been lit in the pubs. Men were standing at the bars speaking an unknown language. It might have been better if I could have spoken it too. I asked for a Scotch and the girl gave me an Edinburgh beer.

"Oh, you mean a whisky," she said when I complained. These were foreign parts.

Near the bus station I found the Roxy Ballroom, and went in. The Teenbeats were on the platform, and on the floor were twisting all the teen-agers of Northumberland, about five scream-ing million of them. All those bottoms, all those squeals, all those silver shellac hairdos; they covered half an acre, winkle-pickers flying, stilettos stomping, and though the Teenbeats had their instruments wired to a dozen loudspeakers they could hardly be heard.

A tall guitarist at the front of the platform, his instrument slung from his hip and swinging above the crowd, leapt in the air with a whoop and flicked his heels like a dancer, and slowly I began to change my mind about Blyth. The girls were so beautiful, chewing their spearmint, their bodies slightly shaking in tight cotton dresses as their limbs flailed about them; idiots they looked, but

32

lovely, innocent idiots. Thirty years ago Priestley lamented the
ugliness of the English people and prophesied that it wouldn't
last; now, thanks to milk in schools or Marks and Spencer or
whatever, they are beautiful, the girls at any rate, even in Blyth. A
young man with side-burns and a long Edwardian coat lined with
scarlet leaned sadly against a pillar; he was ten years out of date.

Outside, a drunk staggered into a derelict house, muttering un-
certainly; after he had gone a laugh rattled down the empty street.
In a passage between the gas-works and the shipyard, fenced in
with old railway sleepers, I overtook a tart on her way to find
work in a dockside pub. A day or two later a town-proud miner
told me that the tarts, as in every other place, always come from
somewhere else; Blyth girls never go on the streets, so tarts come
up from North Shields.

I walked along the quay, under the tall wooden staiths from
which the coal trains tip their loads into the ships — curving
timber viaducts, graceful in the drizzle. The cranes of the shipyard
hung over the river, and a pair of tugs lay side by side, hissing in
the night. Three men were silently fishing, marked by the sudden
glow of their cigarettes. Back in the town I passed a miner going
home, with an old gas-mask case slung across his donkey jacket
and a white enamel billycan in his hand; his face and eyes were
black with coal but his lips were pink, and I had been in Blyth
long enough to know that it meant he had stopped for a beer on
his way.

I mistook my hotel and went into the wrong one, next door;
upstairs a huge woman asked me if she could help, and I mumbled
something and went down and into the right one. In my room
there was coal dust on the window-sill, and for the first time I
noticed the smell of coal in the air.

At breakfast next morning I met Harry, who had also arrived in
Blyth the night before, and I couldn't have been luckier. Harry
was now head waiter of a restaurant in the Tottenham Court Road,
and he was a man of the world. He had been born in Blyth, had
left school at fourteen and gone straight down the pits. Until he
was seventeen he had worked as a driver in charge of the galloways — the pit ponies — but then he had seen the light and gone
away to sea. He had been to the Moscow Trade Fair as a steward,
he had worked at Bush House as a waiter, and now he lived in
Clapham with his Swiss wife. For thirty-four years he had never

been back to Blyth, and he was interested to see if it had changed. The rain had stopped, Harry was going out to look around, and he was happy to take me along.

It was Saturday, and in the market-place they were selling potatoes at ninepence a quarter-stone; cheaper than in Clapham, as Harry said. To show him that he was back in Northumberland they were also selling baskets of bilberries, which he could never buy in Clapham, and he tried to get the stall-holder into conversation. But there was a snag; the local boy, after all these years, was not accepted.

"They're suspicious, these Geordies, you know. I've been away too long." I suggested that it was because of me, a stranger, and we agreed that he should go off on his own, to call on his mother and look up old friends, and meet me again in the evening.

"They're suspicious," repeated an engineer from the new power station, a southerner, later in the day. "Anybody from south of the Trent is just a Londoner to them, and that's the worst thing a man can be. Not with the young people so much, but with the old ones; they remember the thirties, and though they're no longer bitter they still can't give a southerner a welcome. They feel that they have done all the work up here, and the south has made all the money."

Across the Blyth River rose the four white chimneys of his power station—the tallest in the world, so they say in Blyth, and to contradict them would be as dangerous as to insult the local beer. Beer must be more fussed over in Blyth than anywhere else in the world. I met a riveter who on his holiday had taken his car to Devon and found that down there he had been forced to drink cider. Just imagine, a Geordie drinking cider! But nobody in Devon had ever heard of Newcastle beer, and the local stuff was bloody poison.

"They're just lazy," said the town clerk, who came from Hammersmith. "Of course, it's a bit different up here, where you have a whole community devoted to a single industry. A bloke goes off to work with a thousand other men, and when he gets laid off, he finds he's out on the dole with the same thousand. It doesn't encourage him to make an effort. But down south, when a bloke is unemployed his chums help him out until he's found a job again— which makes him find one pretty quickly." It seemed a simple theory.

That Saturday afternoon I walked under the staiths where trains with hundreds of tons of coal rolled across the sky above me, down to the south harbour and along the pier to the lighthouse at the entrance. Anglers – miners perhaps, it's difficult to tell – were casting for mackerel and whiting, and along the beach bathers were splashing in the sunshine. A fleet of fishing-boats from Poland, driven to shelter by a storm in the North Sea, was moored in the basin which, during two world wars, had been a submarine depot, and on the quay round the old brick torpedo house the Polish fishermen were mending their nets; two local girls, tired of walking up and down in front of them, sat down on a bollard and showed their legs, but the Poles, good people's republicans, kept to their nets.

A collier with five thousand tons of coal for a Thames-side power station slipped down to the harbour entrance and into the North Sea, but the men fishing from the pier didn't even look up; they were competing for a prize. Outside the harbour a dinghy race was being held by the Royal Northumberland Yacht Club, with spinnakers and starting-guns and girls in yellow oilskins; and far out to sea, far below the fading collier, far below the sea-bed, men were working in the coal-mines.

*   *   *

Blyth is one of the biggest coal-shipping ports in Europe, handling six million tons a year, and for one glorious year recently it actually was the biggest. Long ago, when Britain exported huge quantities of coal to foreign countries and also to her own coaling stations around the world, most of Blyth's production went abroad. But now almost all the shipments go to British ports, to power stations on the Thames and Medway or along the south coast. Northumberland coal is ideal for power stations, especially in the pulverised state in which it is extracted by modern machinery, and Blyth is banking on its coal continuing to be in demand. Too often, in the early thirties as well as after the last war, the prophets said that coal was doomed, only to be followed a year or so later by a period of record shipments. With no shortage of coal, with colossal demands for electricity, and with new coal-burning power stations, bigger than ever, being built, Blyth has little to worry about.

However Blyth, which has been exporting coal for more than

four hundred years but which has now been declared a scheduled development area, is not content to sit back on its reputation. In a part of the country where affluence is not so general as it might be and where unemployment is a good deal worse than it ought to be, the official slogans of development and diversification are not unheeded; and in spite of a mild complaint that the national conscience is always being directed to the three rivers to the south—the Tyne, Tees and Wear—the authorities of Blyth are determined that the plight of their own river will not be aggravated by its isolation.

A dynamic Harbour Commission, with its eye on two new towns being built north of Newcastle and several new factories being opened in the district—with its eye also on future motorways that could connect exporters in Lancashire, Yorkshire and Scotland through Blyth to their markets in northern Europe— talks about its plans for expansion with confidence, and about its superiority over bigger ports, dogged by labour troubles and chronic congestion, with an almost triumphant pride.

The problem is to decide whether to develop the harbour facilities, which would mean borrowing a lot of money, in order to attract the trade and industry, or wait until the trade and industry are established well enough to justify the expense of developing the harbour. Meanwhile the Commission is making minor improvements, and has plans for modernising the coal loading equipment, to speed up the colliers' turn-round and reduce the costs; eventually the old wooden staiths will be pulled down, to be replaced by a conveyor-belt system that will be more suitable for the bigger colliers that are being introduced. It will be a pity to see the last of the overhead trains pouring coal down a spout into a ship from high above the town, but the old method only loads a ship at the rate of four hundred tons an hour, and rumours have reached Blyth that in America they can load a ship at sixteen thousand tons an hour; that is the way the Harbour Commission means to go. Coal, they say again and again, will only be wanted so long as the price is right.

In a Commission launch I toured the harbour one wet morning, among the gantries and staiths. The sight of a couple of men loading a collier—one controlling the trucks on the ramp of the staith and emptying the coal down the spout, the other standing on deck just watching the hold fill up—made it look the easiest, most economical operation in the world. But the Commission man with me pointed to the other colliers waiting for a berth, and the huge marshalling yards of trucks.

An old dredger was plugging away with its buckets, and an even older ferry-boat hauled itself clanking across the harbour; the special lighter belonging to the new power station was loading ash to be taken out to sea and dumped, and the special lighter belonging to Bates' Colliery, the colliery without a slag-heap, was returning to harbour having sunk its load of stones and rubble; a Trinity House lightship was waiting to be dry-docked, and a pair of blue and white Northumberland cobles were moored alongside a flat-iron, one of the weird hulks that take coal up the Thames and under the London bridges. It was a busy, beautiful scene, even in the rain.

On the south bank of Blyth harbour is a shipyard, not a very big one but it built the world's first aircraft-carrier and it has a name for pioneering new techniques such as prefabrication, even straying from its original function so far as to build the steelwork for road bridges. A new Hoogly River pilot ship was moored off the yard, a second was still on the slip, and the keel of a cargo vessel had just been laid. But shipbuilding orders don't come as fast as they might, and if it wasn't for the yard's five dry docks, which in the summer at least are kept busy repairing ships, the outlook would be bleaker. It is the winter that is dreaded, when the power stations are working at full strength and the colliers are kept at sea.

Across the river on the north side is a ship-breaking yard, where the plates and ribs of Jellicoe's *Thunderer*, Beatty's *Lion*, and Prince Philip's *Magpie* were torn apart to be melted down again in the furnace. I saw the butt end of a cruiser lying on a ramp, a stump of steel like a bit of bone and gristle left at the end of a meal; and a doomed tanker that had already lost its funnel was waiting its turn. Once the breakers get hold of a ship, it doesn't last long; it is tied to a quay for stripping and disembowelling, and then pulled up a tidal basin where the bows are cut off as far as a watertight bulkhead; at successive high tides the dwindling carcase is pulled up again and at low tide another section is cut off and consumed. The operation reminds one of those little fish in South American rivers that attack a man and eat their way steadily through him from one end to the other. The debris lay around the yard, a jungle of chewed-up metal—bits of boiler, davits, pistons, twisted and smashed beyond recognition—with men cracking cast-iron blocks by dropping huge balls on them in a pit, and slicing sheets of steel with flame-cutters. Thousands of tons of scrap waited in the knackery to be turned back into ships, and the only product that was recognisably useful was a small sideline in garden furniture.

*   *   *

That Saturday night I met Harry again and he took me off to the Coronation Club. Clubs, with their bingo evenings and old-time dancing, are more important than pubs in Blyth, and one of the reasons may be that beer costs a shilling and a penny a pint; even 'cellar', a stronger brew, is only one-and-fivepence. At Ashington, a mining town a few miles inland with a population of thirty thousand, there are only three pubs, but more than twenty clubs.

Harry had already penetrated the native suspicion and discovered some old friends; but he had also discovered some things about Blyth that made him not at all regretful that he had left it. At the Coronation he introduced me to his cousin Thomas, an ex-miner who was now deaf and had had to retire to the surface because he could no longer hear the warning sounds of danger at the coal-face; and to George, a huge blond engineman on a mine-shaft winch, who rolled his r's in his throat and used strange Scandinavian words that had to be translated for me.

Harry wouldn't recognise a coal-mine now, they said, and they told him about the diesel trains down below and the pit-head baths on top, while he told me about the old days when he had to walk five miles with his galloways from the shaft bottom, and how he never really washed at all. Bigger extractor fans to bring up the fumes and bigger pumps to drain the water made it a better life, they said, and secretly he said to me that he was beginning to suspect that with the bad old days had gone much of the fine old spirit. Harry was a conservative, and thirty-four years away from Blyth had made him nostalgic for his boyhood years as a driver. The kids used to wear short trousers and be covered in coal—legs and faces and all—and the men all had a hole in their trousers; but now they have baths, and it seemed to have washed more than just the coal off them, and just look at their clothes, said Harry. I looked, and certainly they were dressed in beautiful suits and shirts and ties, with fine pointed shoes and new hats; and their women were magnificent, their hair fresh from the salon, their costume jewellery asparkle, their ruby nails unchipped.

Harry sighed for the miners' whippets and the pigeon races, and for the Sunday morning procession of all the men to a secret place behind the tip at Isabella Colliery where they used to play pitch-and-toss, and where a boy could earn a bob keeping a look-out for the police.

"When did you last play pitch-and-toss behind the 'Bella tip?" he asked his cousin Thomas, and Thomas said it must have been ten years ago, or twenty. Bingo, said Harry, that was the trouble; and you could never lose your week's wages at bingo like you could at pitch-and-toss. All the fun was gone, and all the sorrow.

One thing still remained – the leg shows. I hadn't understood when I heard a reporter on the local paper complain that next Saturday he was going to have to cover thirteen different leg shows; I thought it sounded fun. But in the Coronation Club I saw the notices: Leek Shows. Each club still had its leek show, and many of the pubs. There were to be prizes of six hundred pounds in one of them.

George fetched over another miner, Enoch, a veteran leek grower who could talk about nothing else. The leeks had to be exactly five and a half inches from the button where the roots sprout to the top where the white turns to green, and once they qualified for length it was purely a matter of volume, measured with calipers. Two hundred and thirty-two cubic inches was the record, a leek about a foot thick, but they were good to eat too, Enoch said, if you put them in a pie. I asked him how the leek growers achieved such monsters, but his professional jealousy was too strong, though he must have known I could never compete. George, who was not a leek grower, hinted at milk poured on the roots, and beer, and night-soil, and even witchcraft, but Enoch wasn't telling. What he did admit, though, was the danger from leek slashing. This was the season, just before the leek shows, when the slashers prowled the gardens and allotments of competitors, in the pay of rivals; and hopeful prize-winners had to spend weeks of sleepless nights patrolling with dogs or sitting over their leeks to save them from the slashers' knives.

The year before, Enoch had won a cocktail cabinet with a leek, and with my preconceptions about life in a miner's cottage I asked him what he did with it.

"Fill it," cried Enoch. This year he was after a three-piece bedroom suit, with a double bed.

"Fill it," cried George. We were back on the old subjects of the seaside postcards—booze and sex.

Booze, at any rate round the tables in the Coronation Club lounge where women were allowed, was the main topic, as it was also the main preoccupation. The universal aim of the club's members, to judge from the raffles and competitions with booze for prizes, was more drink at less cost. The men drank pints of 'cellar'—pints and pints of it—and the women drank Advokaat, or alternate cherry brandies and tomato juice. When the men had to go to the lavatory they stopped at the bar, where the women were not allowed, for a large whisky or a liqueur before going back to join the women at the tables; on these occasions George always had two Drambuies.

Sex was not often mentioned, except when George and a plumber and their wives took me upstairs to a room where a 'party' from Newcastle—two singers and a comedian—were giving an entertainment. The singers were dreadful, but I thought the comedian was very funny and I laughed hysterically until I saw that the others were disgusted. But it was not the bawdiness that upset them; it was simply that they had heard all the jokes before, time and again, so we walked out of the room and went back down to the lounge where we could just drink. The plumber even changed his mind about that too, and told his wife that they were going home.

"He's always been temperamental," said George's wife, after they had gone.

Blyth is a man's town, and perhaps the reason is that it is almost entirely a working-class town. There is only a very small middle class ("Not a Jew in the place," the town clerk said) to corrupt the women with ideas of self-importance. Even in the days before the nationalisation of coal, when the mines were private, the rich families tended to live inland, up in the lovely Northumberland countryside, while Blyth always remained industrial and working class. That may be why the women are kept in their place. In the newest, finest club in the town, the Comrades' Club, an additional room has recently been added, with splendid wooden panelling, deep upholstered chairs, and immense vases of plastic flowers that are changed every other month to keep up with the season; it is the Male Lounge, and women are forbidden to enter.

In the Coronation Club that Saturday night George, full of beer and Drambuie and sentiment, seized another miner and went up to the platform where there was a microphone and a man doodling on an electric organ. Together they crooned about their hearts ever faithful, their love ever true, with their arms round each other as though they meant it. The salt of the earth, you might call them, or nature's gentlemen, or just a couple of boozy miners. We all cheered, and the club secretary gave them each a packet of cigarettes. Their performance encouraged another singer, a young pit-head costing clerk, who squeezed the microphone and sang a very personal dirge about the Mona Lisa. The organist could accompany anything without the music, and knew just when to swell or fade, and when to fill in if the soloist forgot his lines.

I hoped the miners would talk about their work and their pay, but they were reluctant. George, a surface worker who had only been down below half a dozen times in forty years at the pit, said he usually brought home nine or ten pounds in his weekly packet, which I expect was a deliberate underestimate, for my benefit or for his wife; the average wage for colliery workers in Northumberland is nearly seventeen pounds a week, with a free or almost free house thrown in and a free supply of coal. The face-workers, the fillers who actually get the coal from the seam and who are the aristocrats of the pits as well as the highest paid, were the most reticent; a middle-aged man with a slim, strong body but with blue scars under the white skin of his face – a strange mixture of healthy unhealth – would only talk about all the deductions from his weekly earnings, for union subscription, taxes and the miners' welfare fund. It was not until I went to a coal-face myself that I learnt the fillers were getting twenty-four pounds, and anybody who sees the work would probably agree that they are underpaid.

A subject they were all, especially the older men, anxious to talk about was the National Coal Board's policy of training young miners – a policy that they mostly disapproved of. Nowadays there is no question of a boy leaving school and going straight down the pit, as Harry had done. Everybody is given intensive specialist training; and old hands like George, for instance, thought it was a waste of time, all this education and sending miners to college. But then George was intolerant of anything new-fangled, and nothing horrified him more than when the old wash-house at his pit, where the coal is sprayed and sorted before being shipped away, was re-named the Coal Preparation Plant.

The singers went on until closing-time, rounded off by a special solo from a Salvation Army man, and then 'God Save the Queen'. I thought I had got off lightly, with only four pints of 'cellar' and two whiskies, and when I bumped into Harry outside and he pointed to his pockets bulging with bottles and tried to persuade me to come on to a party at the other end of town, I resisted.

Next morning, as I was going out to buy a Sunday paper after breakfast, I met him coming home, with a puffed and horrible pallor on his unshaven face, no tie, and stories of gin and whisky and half a bottle of rum that he had had to leave behind. But alcohol wasn't his only trouble that morning. Harry was disappointed with Blyth.

"It seems that if you haven't got a bloody bingo card in your hand you're not doing anything in Blyth now. Nobody thinks for themselves any more, it's all done for them. I haven't had an intelligent conversation since I came. As if juke-boxes in the pubs aren't bad enough. All the time, it's heads down for the old clickety-click. Christ, it makes you disgusted. They'll soon be taking them up to the cemetery, clutching their bingo cards."

Harry was disappointed, and he was also sad for his old town. As a head waiter in London he was far richer than most of his contemporaries who had stayed at home, even men with a skilled trade who had done five years' apprenticeship; an old friend of his, a riveter with a wife and three children, had lost his job in the shipyard years ago and was now helping to put up new street lights in the town, for eight pounds ten a week; it made Harry weep, he said. And the pettiness of Blyth life, and the silly feuds; even in his old home there was a row—a bull-and-cow he called it, in the rhyming slang he had picked up in London—going on between his cousin and his aged mother. The only thing he approved of was the way everybody still contributed to the funds for charity; a cut from every lottery, raffle and bingo session, he said, went to old miners or their widows, and to Harry that was the only sign of the old spirit of his Blyth.

But he had seen enough; he was taking the night train to London; tomorrow he would be home in Clapham, the next day he would be back at his restaurant in the Tottenham Court Road, and it would be another thirty-four years before he came back to Blyth.

*   *   *

I stayed on, and went down a coal-mine. A 'pit' is a more expressive word, and the one they use in Blyth. Everybody has a good idea what it's like to go down a coal-mine, but that doesn't make it any nicer. Bates' Colliery, the mine which I went down at Blyth and which had its first shaft sunk in 1798, had been recently modernised by the National Coal Board and now produces more than three thousand tons of coal a day with less than two thousand men, but that doesn't make it much nicer, either. The pleasantest part of Bates' is the surface; being at the edge of Blyth harbour, which means that the coal can be loaded straight from the top of the shaft into the ships and the slag and stones can be easily taken out to sea and dumped, it has a special advantage over inland mines; and it is not surprising that the lawns and geranium beds round its new pit-head buildings have earned it a prize for the best-kept colliery. But none of this makes a journey to the coal-face, more than seven hundred feet down to the bottom of the shaft and then three miles horizontally under the sea, exactly a pleasure.

There are now thirty-seven coal-mines working in Northumberland, which is less than half the number at the time they were nationalised, and in another ten years they may be halved again. The Coal Board is not worried about the future supply of coal or the future demand for it so long as the price is competitive, and the policy in Northumberland is to close down the smaller, uneconomical mines and develop a few of the big ones, like Bates'. As the working faces of the coal seams recede further from the pit shafts — and usually further out to sea — the coal becomes more expensive to bring out, but the increasing cost is met with increasing efficiency and mechanisation, and although the total coal production remains more or less constant, it is achieved with fewer men employed in fewer pits. This means that there are now more miners than are really needed, and with compulsory retirement at sixty-five old miners are only being replaced by men transferred from pits that have been closed down, or by the handful of boys that the Coal Board recruits each year to keep a proper balance among the age groups.

Certainly this policy has aggravated the unemployment rate in the district, which is more than twice the national average. Many of the villages round Blyth where small mines were closed down have been badly hit, and in a tight mining community where there is no tradition of emigration there is now the prospect of the sons and grandsons of miners wanting to work in the pits but being unable to get jobs.

I arrived at the manager's office at nine in the morning, and was told that we would be going down in forty minutes, with the back-shift. I was given a denim boiler-suit, gum-boots, rubber knee-pads, a leather belt, a cotton scarf and a helmet. It made me feel very much like a miner, and I thought I must also look like one, but when I caught sight of myself in the office mirror I saw that I just looked rather foolish.

With the group manager, a trade union official and an overman —authentic miners, all of them—I was marched down a corridor and into a room where we were given electric lamps to fix on our helmets, with heavy batteries slung on our leather belts. Then we joined the crowd that was converging on the shaft.

Everybody explained to me what was happening, but I was very confused. The discipline of preparation for the descent, and the inevitability of dropping into the darkness on a wire from a wheel spinning in the sky, drove me to wild, unreasonable fears; this is what it must be like, I thought, on the scaffold. I tried to tell myself that it was not only my ordeal, and that there were hundreds of men with me who did this every day; but it was difficult to remember that I was among men who were on their way to an ordinary day's work, for through the atmosphere of cheerful efficiency stretched a tense feeling of nervousness, a kind of half-acknowledged fatalism, that would not exist among workers going into a factory or an office. The miners were talking and laughing, but they were also being very serious—as who wouldn't be, who was going a long way down into the ground and then a much longer way horizontally under the sea, there to spend eight hours doing one of the most gruelling and dangerous jobs ever per-formed by men.

Suddenly in the crowd I caught sight of George, clocking in for his shift in the winch engine-house. With the desperation of a man about to leave the world for ever, I broke away from our little party to shake his hand. He grinned in surprise and said something

I was too overwhelmed to hear, and the manager asked me gruffly where I had met him.

We passed through a succession of concrete rooms divided by iron doors with notices about contraband, and as each door clanked the changing pressure popped in my ears. The overman gave me two metal tabs, one square and one round, and told me to put the round one in a tin and keep the square one in my pocket until I came up from the pit; but I never saw the tin and kept both tabs, and when I came up three hours later he was offended that the system hadn't worked. We were carefully frisked for contraband—matches and inflammable objects—and then we were being directed, like sheep going into a double-decker railway truck, into the cage. Eighteen of us stood in the dark, and the last man pulled the netting gate down. My helmet touched the roof. Almost immediately there was a rush of cool air and we were shuddering, rattling downwards.

At the bottom I found that nothing very dreadful had happened to me, and I assumed an air of blasé nonchalance; I would show them that no coal-mine could hold any surprises for me now. We walked along a tunnel with strip lighting overhead, like the London underground but without advertisements. The men of the fore-shift were walking the other way, dirty and noisy, and the two shifts shouted greetings at each other. The manager showed me a panel of cement in the wall scratched with the name of Hugh Gaitskell, to mark his visit to Bates' Colliery when he was Minister of Fuel and Power. We got into a little diesel train and drove on further into the tunnel, out of the strip lighting and into the darkness.

"That's the low tide mark," said the manager, flashing his lamp on the ribs of the tunnel, and I tried to think of the beach and the Polish fishing-boats above me. There was a sudden smell, strong and familiar but anachronistic, which for a moment I couldn't place. "The stables," said the overman, rather aggressively. "I like it. Good farmyard smell." I think I had vaguely believed that pit ponies were no longer used, and I felt a little indignant at learning I was wrong, as though the truth had been deliberately kept from me. Perhaps, after all, Harry would not have found a modern coal-mine so unfamiliar. Later, whenever we came to a pony pulling a truck, the overman would stop and make me admire it. A pony's life was a joy these days, he said, a real joy; and he would pat its flanks and show how there wasn't a trace of sweat, and I would sneeze at the cloud of coal dust that rose from its coat. They have food fit for racehorses, he said, and a special cat in their stables to catch the mice that come down in the hay; they're spoilt nowadays, the pit ponies, and I got the impression that every horse in England secretly wants to work down a coal-mine.

The train stopped at several points to drop parties of miners off; they slung their haversacks over their shoulders and disappeared down 'gates', the small tunnels leading from the main road to the coal-face. About three miles from the shaft we too got off and disappeared down our own gate, while the train rumbled on along the main road with its dwindling load of passengers.

We walked for another half-mile over the uneven sleepers of a track, sometimes splashing through water, sometimes stooping for a few paces where the roof came too low. The overman pointed out electric cables, machines, pumps, telephones, first-aid posts, stretchers. He dialled a number on a telephone and gave me the receiver, to show that it really worked; the voice at the other end was a man in the pit-head office where I had left my clothes.

For a few minutes we walked through the thick smell of explosive, but the overman said it wouldn't last and soon we were in fresh air again. This was one of the surprises of the day—the cool clean air. I had expected a foul atmosphere of heat and gas and dust, but down here, seven hundred feet below the surface and three miles from the pit shaft, it was fresher than in a London street. I wondered why the exhausts of cars and buses and lorries are not treated in the same way as the diesel engines in a coal-mine, to obliterate the fumes. Apart from an occasional whiff of explosives the sharpest smell was when we passed a pony pulling a truck along the rails.

We reached the end of the gate, a stone wall in front of us blocking the tunnel, with no escape. The stone wall, however, didn't rest on the ground. At its foot there was a horizontal gap stretching the width of the tunnel, thirty-two inches high and kept open with vertical wooden props. I squatted and looked in, and saw a man rolling energetically about between the floor and the roof of the gap, with his helmet lamp flashing among the props. I recognised him as a filler; I realised that I was looking at a coal-face; and I thought that my journey was over. Nothing to it, it seemed, though I was glad I wasn't the man lying down there.

"That's the Beaumont Seam," said the overman. "There's another seam, the Plessey, a hundred feet above us."

I think now that he and the trade unionist and the group manager all believed that I knew what I was in for; at any rate they didn't tell me, and I'm glad they didn't. For we were going to get down into that gap, that seam two and a half feet high from which the coal was being mined, and we were going to wriggle along in it for a distance of a hundred and twenty-five yards, from the tunnel of the tail-gate to the tunnel of the main-gate. If I had known it, the prospect of crawling through a narrow coal seam for such a distance and in such a situation would have been awful, as is the recollection; and only the actual experience was sufficiently preoccupying for me to have scarcely time to ponder its implications.

The overman dived down into the gap, squirmed between a pair of props, and turned at right angles to the tunnel we had come down. I followed his boots. In a few seconds my hands and wrists were black.

Almost immediately the thud of an explosion filled the air, and the pressure of it pushed against my face. The overman shouted, and somebody far ahead shouted back. I had no idea what was going on, until the overman told me he had told the miners not to do any more detonating while we were at the face. We wriggled on.

A few inches to my left was the loose coal that had been shattered by detonations, and a few inches to the right was a moving conveyor belt, running to the main-gate. The fillers, ten men spread along the hundred and twenty-five yards between the gates, were shovelling coal from the face to the belt. They were doing this in a space thirty-two inches high, constricted by pit props every two or three feet; and they were doing it at the rate of two tons each an hour, or fifteen tons a shift. Those ten men between them were bringing out seven hundred and fifty tons of coal a week, an achievement that would be prodigious in any conditions, and which, down here, was so staggering that their twenty-four pounds a week were quite irrelevant.

Every day that shift of ten fillers advanced four feet through the seam, along their hundred and twenty-five yard front, drilling holes for their explosives, shovelling the broken coal on to the belt, and shoring up the rock roof with props. And every day men in other shifts prepared the new face, moved the conveyor-belt four feet forward, and pulled the old pits props out from where the coal had been removed, to let the rock roof collapse on to the rock floor.

Between the smooth rock under me and the smooth rock above me I found that, where there was not too much coal about on the floor, I could usually just crawl; otherwise I had to straighten out my legs and wriggle. The thought of hundreds of feet of rock on top of me, brushing my spine and nudging my helmet, with another seam being worked somewhere above me, and then the sea-bed and the fish and ships and waves, was so absurd that I couldn't really entertain it. More palpable was the sight, behind the conveyor belt, of infinite tons of broken rock, where the props had been pulled out after the coal had been mined and the roof had subsided on to the floor; the idea of all that weight was difficult to grasp, but it made me careful about wriggling round the wooden props.

This was the source of everything. This was where industry begins. This was coal, but also electricity and gas — one of the ingredients of every man-made thing we see as we look around a room or walk along a street, one of the essences of our prosperity, one of the origins of our power. Almost nothing tangible exists in our civilisation that hasn't, in some way and at some stage, been subjected to coal. Coal affects every minute of our lives, and these men were getting it for us.

This too was what Blyth was all about. On my first evening a week earlier I had been unable to find the centre of the town, and here was the reason. The cramped coal-faces of its collieries are the nub of Blyth in a way that no High Street or market-place could ever be. Down in this pit, perhaps at this very coal-face, the mayor of Blyth himself was working, and one of his aldermen and three of his councillors. It didn't matter that in a few hours' time they would be prancing naked into the new pit-head showers, that tomorrow they would be debating the civic budget and putting up the rates, that next summer they would be holidaying on the Costa Brava. Here they were now, black and sweating and lying in a crevice hundreds of feet underground, several miles out to sea, shovelling coal.

IV

LEEK

THE view from the Morridge, at the western edge of the moors, is terrific. Far beyond the pall of Stoke-on-Trent and the slag-heaps of the Potteries one can see the Wrekin and the misty Welsh hills, and to the north-west the improbable blur of Jodrell Bank telescope; to one's left are the rolling fields of Staffordshire, and on a hill to the right stands a tall futuristic tower—whether for tracking every missile that leaves the ground in Central Asia or just for putting out the B.B.C. it's difficult to tell; at one's back the moors stretch to Derbyshire and the Peak, with the ghostly scar of a huge cement works and scattered ancient farmsteads where often the hay-rakes are pulled by horses and the cows are milked by hand; and at one's feet, under a veil of smoke pierced by a score of slender chimneys, lies the Queen of the Moorland: Leek.

Macclesfield, Congleton, Leek—of the trio of textile towns on the border of Staffordshire and Cheshire Leek is the least well-known outside the district, though with twenty thousand inhabitants it is about the size of Penzance, or Chichester, or Buxton. Being a typical English town, dependent for its living on its own industry and the agriculture of the district, it is possessed of typical English paradoxes—a left-wing Labour Member of Parliament and a right-wing Urban District Council, a mild reputation for non-conformism and no possible likelihood of starting any sort of a revolution; and being in an isolated position, 'twelve miles from everywhere' as the Leekensians say, it has preserved its individuality more completely than the other towns of North Staffordshire and the Cheshire plain.

The trouble with Leek, if there can be any trouble with a place of such consummate ordinariness, is that its industry is as conservative as the surrounding agriculture, and since the Huguenots first started weaving silk there in the seventeenth century nothing more memorable has happened in its history than the decision of a number of Victorian ladies to stitch a replica of the Bayeux tapestry. Even the Young Pretender, passing through Leek in 1745, hardly bothered to plunder it. Its tradition of stout conservatism, as in so many industrial market-towns of England, has modelled Leek's character and then cast it beyond change, and although the mills and markets have not brought great hardship to the people, neither have they brought great prosperity.

"Why pick on Leek?" asked a girl in the office of the *Leek Post and Times*, half apologetic for her home-town's mediocrity, half indignant that I should come and investigate it; Leek had never done anything to anybody, and who did I think I was, breezing in from London and rootling in the dust?

"Why Leek?" echoed a man in the bar of the Roebuck. "Look" —he pointed to an elderly customer with a tweed fisherman's hat and a kindly twinkle—"that fellow just about sums up Leek. Old-fashioned. He runs a chemist's, but I don't believe he knows the difference between an anti-biotic and a bloody anti-aircraft gun."

Old-fashioned was a word I often heard in Leek, which may have denoted an encouraging concern with the state of things, but from old people it probably just meant nostalgia, and from young people it all too often just indicated a sense of bitterness. However in many respects, particularly for a visitor, it's nice that Leek is still the way it is.

Up in the square every Tuesday night stalls are set up for Wednesday's market, and although recently the cattle market has been removed from the centre of the town to make way for a new block of shops and a supermarket is already open in the main street, most of the ironmongers and greengrocers seem to have resisted the advance of packaged goods and plastic display stands, and have the same air of unchangeability, inside and out, as most of the gaunt red-brick mills. The mills themselves bear grand historic names—Waterloo, Wellington, Nelson, Albion; and the names of the old mill-owning families—Wardle, Tatton, Nicholson—are still spoken in the tone of familiarity, part affection and part resentment, that marks a working man's special feeling for the firm that has employed him and his people for generations, even though in many cases the old family has now left the business.

Along the narrow streets between the mills—surprisingly clean and unsmoky to someone who thinks of an industrial town as a vast accretion of filth—the oak-grained doors of mill-workers' cottages are kept polished, and glossy prams glint through the nylon curtains of front parlour windows. Old men sit at the foot of the hideous war memorial, saying nothing, while their wives eat potato crisps. 'Turn to Christ' advises a sticker on the back of a car, a banner across a shopping street advertises the Leekensian Amateur Operatic Society in a performance of *Iolanthe*, and in a stationer's window black-edged notices of funerals invite friends to accept this as the only intimation. The cortège, they add, will leave the deceased's house at two-thirty, and I watched a splendid one pass down Saint Edward's Street, in front of the lovely Georgian houses that now belong to solicitors and building societies; like a bullock among sheep, one of the big gravel lorries that ply between the Moorland and the Potteries had got mixed up with the undertaker's old black saloons and was crawling with them patiently; but a great blue Jaguar, a rarity in Leek, lost its temper and shot up a steep cobbled street for a short-cut behind a factory.

"A typical mill is an old-fashioned mill," said a young journalist, speaking for his generation. One of the mills in Leek, he told me, still makes its own bobbins, apparently oblivious that specialist factories can now do a better, cheaper job and let the mill get on with its own work. He complained too that the mills never co-operate on experiments or research, but jealously keep their secrets from each other.

I saw what he meant when I sat in the cosy office of the manager of a mill that made 'textile smallwares'—shoelaces, braids, knitted goods—and heard him disclaim any fears of competition from Hong Kong or Japan. Nothing had ever upset them in the past, and he couldn't see that anything ever would. Of course, he said, it was different up in Lancashire, where many mills had had to close down, but not being a cotton town, Leek had nothing to worry about, and anyway it had a tradition of fair-mindedness to the workers and unions which would always ensure that everyone made a good living. Of developments in the industry he said that there were a lot more of these synthetics about nowadays, but they were not considered as innovations so much as simply new ways of making the old things. As I left he added that, come to think of it, there was some good stuff coming from Italy these days; and he shuddered slightly as we shook hands.

The journalist's complaint was common. So, among ambitious

young men I talked to, was a dissatisfaction about their prospects in Leek. Too often, they felt, the mills were owned by families that passed control from father to son and naturally reserved the best positions for themselves; other responsible jobs were given to men who had worked faithfully up from the bottom, but who had no technical qualifications beyond their experience. Anybody with ambition had to go to Stoke or the Potteries, where there was more variety, more scope, and more money.

"The mills are feudal," said a young man with an economics degree from Exeter university, in the Jazz Club one night. I had heard the noise coming from a top window of the George, and went up to see what was going on. A five-piece band roared in a corner, while pretty girls in trousers and young men in sweaters danced in the wild half-dark. With bottles hanging from the ceiling and a bar decorated black and hung with bull-fighting posters from Spain, the club contrived to be as un-Leek as possible. Everybody seemed to be under twenty-five, and in one way or another, from a history graduate who wanted to get an M.A. and then teach at Liverpool to two girls who were talking vaguely about Australia, everybody seemed to be trying to get away. Only a young farmer from the neighbourhood, drinking at the bar and ogling the dancers, found all he wanted in that den above the George; he was born in Leek and he wouldn't live anywhere else.

The next morning I asked the secretary of the local trade union if the mills were really as antique as the Jazz Club believed, and he replied, "Only some of them." He complained that many of them had been miserably slow to introduce proper incentive schemes for the workers, but two or three had started off and the rest were gradually, perhaps reluctantly, following.

The longer I stayed in Leek the more I felt that those young men were mistaken about their town, and that it was they who were out of touch with the times. For centuries Leek was a silk town, but for a long time now it has hardly produced any silk at all. Fifty years ago one of the mills in the town made the first rayon stockings, and since then the emphasis has changed from spinning to clothes-making, dyeing and the processing of artificial fibres. So far from being the ghost town that the Jazz Club lamented, it is probably as prosperous as it ever has been, and its businessmen a great deal more enterprising than their predecessors.

As a sentimental traveller I found myself in a quandary, half
regretting the crumbling of the old pattern of small family
businesses gently basking in picturesque buildings, half excited at
the vision of their successors and the astonishing new processes
for man-made fibres. The valued old business connections that
had been cherished over the years have now given way to sales
trips to Milan and California; the old Leek families have been
joined—or ousted—by new Leek men, and by Lancashiremen,
Yorkshiremen, Londoners, Jews, and in several cases the business
has been floated as a public company; the handsome brick buildings that sufficed for so long have had flimsy additions built on,
with bigger windows and more space; the worn wooden floors
have been stripped of their clattering old machinery and spread
with high-speed monsters; the hanks of fine silk, the best in the
world, have become cartons of drip-dry synthetics and delicious,
trembling piles of nylon undies.

With so much flux in the industry, with an industry that is itself
so precarious, and perhaps with a few blunders to remember, it is
not surprising that Leek is always full of rumours. Somebody says
that one of the biggest mills, the very one that pioneered artificial
silk stockings and for many years the solidest in town, is now in
difficulties and is shutting down one department after another;
somebody else says that another mill in the centre of Leek that
was bought up recently by a big Lancashire firm and has already
sold half of its premises is now offering the other half to the town
council for a car park, threatening the livelihood of many hundreds of employees; and somebody says he went to Italy for his
summer holidays this year and bought a silk scarf there for five
bob that was better than anything made in Leek, and he won't be
having a holiday at all next year because the whole town will be
out on its ear. But anybody can see, from visiting half a dozen
factories if not from Leek's unemployment rate which is one of
the lowest in England, that it is far from the sink of doom that its
more frustrated inhabitants make it out to be.

Happily, Leek at the moment has something of both ages.
There are still a few of the old firms, founded a century or two
ago by the ancestors of the present owner and struggling to adapt
themselves to a faster, cruder world. It may be that they will
survive, or else they will close down, or be bought up by a bigger
neighbour; they sometimes give the impression that they

themselves don't know which is most probable, nor which most preferable. Meanwhile they function efficiently but not particularly lucratively, which is more or less what they did a hundred years ago; the difference is that the products and the machinery have altered, and in the little yard by the office where a carriage used to stand there is now a car, though not a very expensive one.

Typical of the old school of Leek businessmen was the chairman of the Urban District Council, a magistrate and a formidable elder of Leek who had been a Methodist preacher since he was fifteen. I met him in his factory, a small dyeworks with two or three dozen workers that had remained almost unchanged since it was started by his father. The boss seemed to be working in both the office and the dyehouse at once; in a shirt with no collar and the stud undone, he was, as he said himself, probably the only Justice of the Peace in England to be wearing wooden clogs. His family had worn clogs for three hundred years, but this was his last pair and he couldn't get any more. His other concern was the decline of Methodism; otherwise, he was not very worried about anything. But something did suggest that he was beginning to feel the pressure of less archaic firms, and he admitted that he was contemplating a gesture of condescension to progress: "People say I'm too old to give up hand-dyeing," he said defiantly, "but I say I'm not."

I couldn't help thinking of a farmer I had visited up on the Moorland a few days earlier. For eighty pounds a year he rented forty acres of grazing, which was more than most of his neighbours had, and he owned a tractor and a milking-machine which set him far above many of them, but it seemed that he was doing well if he made more than five pounds a week. Now that his eldest son had left school and could help him on the farm he was trying to find a bigger place, but a fifty-acre farm in the district had recently been sold for over three thousand pounds and that was more than he could ever afford. Meanwhile he and his wife and six children were living in an old stone farmhouse twelve hundred feet above sea-level in conditions that could scarcely have altered since the house was built. The floor of their kitchen was awash with an indeterminable liquid which children and chickens shared with an electric washing-machine, a startling object among such squalor and about the only feature in the scene that placed it in the twentieth century. The wife offered me a cup of tea, but squeamishness overcame me and with shame I declined.

The chairman of the council in his clogs, mixing his own dyes and talking about John Wesley as though he passed through Leek only last week, marks the last generation of the men who ran Leek's industry for a century and a half. The other extreme was epitomised by a German who, with his father, had started making light clothing just before the war, and now owned several factories and was considered one of the best employers in the town, although I suspect he was still not entirely accepted by Leek society and probably didn't care much for it anyway. Since a delegate from a new African country had flipped through his catalogue and ordered an arbitrary fifty samples of each model, he was prepared for anything, and that very morning a big order had arrived from Russia for cotton underclothes; it more than paid for his stand at the British Trade Fair in Moscow.

He took me through some of his departments, full of the noise of sewing-machines and Workers' Playtime, where girls with their hair in curlers and their machines draped with close-up shots of the pop singers they dreamed about, were stitching away at mountains of pink and yellow panties. Overhead swung placards — Margaret, Alexandra, Anne, Marina — and the German explained that his girls were arranged in teams, each under the name of a royal princess.

"As a boy I went to nine different schools. One of them was an English public school, and there I learnt the value of the house spirit." By way of apology he introduced me to a girl who had just come back from a design course in New York, to show that not only the forces of reaction ruled his firm.

Another man with an international outlook was the managing director of a big dyeing and printing works employing many hundreds of workers, a public company with a thoroughly up-to-date plant. Having started at the bottom and risen to control it, although not a member of the family whose august name the firm still carried, he ridiculed the idea that there were no prospects for ambitious young men in Leek; the trouble was, he said, that too often his company had offered opportunities of technical courses and further education to young men who had failed to honour their share of the bargain, and instead of giving up time for study they had spent it in pubs and cinemas. Otherwise there was nothing—least of all nepotism—to stop them doing what he had done.

Apart from one or two businesses and the ordinary commercial, professional and administrative activities of a small town, there is nothing for anybody wanting to escape from textiles but the early morning bus to Stoke or the Potteries. But although the pay is better in the Potteries the conditions are worse, and many working people prefer to go into the textiles factories—men into the dye-works and women into the mills—because the work is compara-tively clean and light. In a pub one night I met an old master baker who gave up baking years ago and got an unskilled job in a mill where he could earn more than he ever did even in charge of a bakery. The landlord leant over the bar: "Ay, and it took a bit of getting used to, Henry, didn't it? After all those years' baking you used to get up at three in the morning and wander through the streets looking for an oven, remember? And by eleven you were ready to knock off and come in here for a pint."

The landlord himself, a colossal man with a capacity of many gallons, was too good a target for his customers to miss. They said he had a little car, and when he got out of it the car would rise up about eighteen inches off the road and scratch itself, "like a woman getting out of her corsets". But in his pub I learnt some-thing of the murkier happenings of Leek, related with relish and not a little pride. It was all very well for us fellows down in London, they told me, thinking we had everything, what with Profumo and the Argylls and all that; but here in Leek nothing would ever surprise them; their own material was just as good.

Indeed, it would be utterly wrong to suppose that the people of Leek are dissatisfied. Coming from the south I was impressed by the town's self-sufficiency and its self-respect; not parochial, still less complacent, I felt it had a more positive identity than a southern town.

"They *like* Leek," said a social worker who had come from Lancashire and grown to like it too. He was appalled at some of the things he found, particularly in the countryside, and he re-sented the fortune that was being spent on developing Africa and Asia when it was so badly needed in his district; but he also resented any suggestion that it was a backwater.

Gently Leek, like its textile mills, is waking up; and most of its people, instead of rushing to the big cities, are happy to stay in

Leek. For entertainment, now that one of its three cinemas has been burnt down and another converted into 'Staffordshire's friendliest bingo hall', anybody wanting more than amateur dramatics or an exhibition of Japanese woodcuts on loan to the public library may find Leek a bit barren; though in fact there is a flourishing arts club, and even an art school which, besides full-time students and employees sent by the mills to learn designing, attracts amateur painters, sculptors, and potters in astonishing numbers. But passenger trains no longer run to Leek station, and even the football special that survived them for a few seasons has now been stopped; so Stoke City supporters have to crowd on to buses, or stay at home and watch the television.

"Or bingo," said a greengrocer scathingly. His wife, he said, preferred the cinema with bingo to the one with films; there was no cat-calling from the youths in front, no smooching at the back, and she could feel she was really taking part in something, not just being entertained. To get her away, he was going to buy a car, like a lot of other husbands; he hoped she would like boasting about driving to the pictures in the Potteries, and on a sunny weekend they could join all the other picnickers up on the Moorland.

Holidays too have changed their pattern, and although there are still hundreds of Leekensians who have hardly ever left the town except to go to Rhyl or Blackpool, there is a growing number who are more adventurous. A travel agency that opened a few years ago can take much of the credit for breaking the old habits; from mill-girls going on a seventeen-guinea trip to Austria to elderly parents visiting their G.I.-bride daughter in America, or even to retired couples cruising round the world on their savings, Leek is cautiously stirring abroad. An organised tour to Majorca is easily the favourite, and the agency can now fill a special chartered plane; most of the passengers are either middle-aged married couples or young unmarried couples, and the manager is hard put to it to keep his customers' secrets.

A contemporary coffee-bar, next to a fish and chip shop, is an obvious result; every night it is crammed with teen-agers and young mill-workers — a much more lively place than the only other good restaurant, a dolled-up pub with French waiters and expensive food, with walls cluttered with coach-horns and warming-pans, with faint music from behind the miniature liqueur

bottles, and with Annigoni's Queen looking wearily down on all
the gin-and-tonics. The customers there are rarely Leek people,
but visiting businessmen on expense accounts who are inclined to
talk loudly about the last time they were driving from Zürich to
Bologna. The customers in the coffee-bar, many of whom have
been abroad too, talk just as loudly, but nobody listens.

The picture of Leek—all too easy to deduce from the view of
the town from the Morridge—as a sleepy old place fraught with
introspection and in-breeding is deceptive. During the Napoleonic
Wars it housed a camp of French prisoners, many of whose
descendants survive in the town, their names adapted to the
Staffordshire accent; and after the last war it suffered a similar
influx of Polish refugees, most of whom have now been absorbed,
professionally and socially. Leek is used to innovations, and
though I don't believe there is yet a black man in the place, except
on Wednesdays when some of the market stalls are erected by
Asians and Africans, it is no longer the tight little community it
used to be. The evolution is not entirely due to the crumbling of
the old hierarchy; when a factory manager said to me, "It all boils
down to the operative," he was referring to the efficiency of his
new machinery, but he might just as well have been talking
about the whole town of Leek.

v

LUDLOW

The last days of October, soft and warm and golden in London, drove me to the hills; to the Clee Hills in particular, for I had never been there, and there were others not far away—Wenlock Edge, the Long Mynd, the Wrekin, the Forest of Clun—with odd, abrupt names and the promise of good walking. I decided to walk first over the Clees from Bridgnorth to Ludlow.

There was no longer a train to Bridgnorth, and I had to go to Wolverhampton, twelve miles away, and then take a bus. Wolverhampton, for half an hour between the train and the bus, was the ugliest town I can remember: a disgusting canal with scum in the corners, grime-blackened buildings, huge peeling bill-boards—even the town centre seemed to be just a façade for endless factories, a reluctant gesture for convention's sake. A magnificent African with a bow-tie and a bowler hat and carrying a rolled umbrella was the happiest thing in sight; the other people were as cheerless as the streets.

From the top of the bus the autumn afternoon looked bleakly unpromising. Lorries full of muddy turnips rocked out of the fields on to the road, and a creeping mist solemnly wiped out the colours. But then, without warning, the bus lurched over the edge of the Severn valley and ground in low gear down to the river. It was Bridgnorth.

Bridgnorth lies on both banks of the river, with a Low Town on the east and a High Town on the west. It is the High Town that is the glory and the surprise of the place, with a unique hill-top flavour that is quite un-English. The castle is only a lolling fragment surrounded by flower-beds and a war memorial, but that afternoon Saint George's cross flew from the tower of the red sandstone church and the pubs were open for the people who had come to market. There was a feeling of Italy in the air, and a general benevolence.

"That's the village I come from," said the girl in the hotel where I booked in, when I gave my name.

"How d'ye do?" said an old man I bumped into, going round a corner.

"Eileen is a fool," said a scrawl chalked on the wall of one of the steep flights of steps down to the river, and somebody had added, "Very true."

"Gladys!" shouted a woman in a doorway down an empty street, but something about her tone of voice suggested she didn't expect anybody to answer. I tried to think who "the learned and eloquent Richard Baxter" was, who had once lived in a house near the church; I slithered down mossy steps two hundred feet to the river, looked into caves in the sandstone cliffs that seemed to have been quite recently inhabited, and came up again, for fivepence, alone in a funicular; and I found myself in a darkening alley of such weird, silent atmosphere, with the lights going up in the window of an old-fashioned watchmaker and a family tailor's shop offering heavy corduroy suits, that I almost wondered whether I had really been in London, in 1963, that same morning.

But it was the food shops—the butchers and pork-pie raisers and greengrocers—that enthralled me most. There was a genuineness about them, after London shops, that was irresistible, and I found it hard not to go in and buy those good things. There were pork scratchings at sixpence a pound, and faggots, and home-killed beef, and home-made brawn and lard and dripping in moulded shapes, and ravishing pies differing from shop to shop, and carrots still smelling of earth, and great pale cabbages, and pears and apples from local orchards lying open to the soft Shropshire air. It was a long way from the pre-packed meat of London butchers and their dismal displays of packets of instant stuffing, and the greengrocers' polythened and frozen vegetables.

But for dinner in the hotel there were tinned beans and peas with my steak, and no fresh fruit at all, though afterwards there were compensations. A troupe of amateur actors with guns and Texan hats filled the bar with incredible hilarity, until they retired to some distant annexe and rocked the building far into the night with Frankie and Johnny and songs of that Swannee shore. And a splendid black girl dressed in a white cap and apron came into my room and popped a hot-water bottle into my bed. For a moment I thought she was going to pop in herself.

*   *   *

In the morning I tried to find a bus that would take me to Cleobury North, a village seven miles away under the Brown Clee. I was directed to a stuffy little room above a hairdresser's, where one of the Texans of the night before was sitting with a girl at a telephone switchboard, while another girl, a very pretty one, hovered at an ironing board on the landing outside. We made a lot of telephone calls around the town, and discovered that the early morning school bus had already gone and there was nothing else before the evening school bus. So I walked.

It was a misty morning, but dry, and I thought it would turn fine later. I left the last house behind, and the end of the speed limit, and came to the first milestone — Bridgnorth 1, Ludlow 18; then the second, and the third. There was no sign of the Clee Hills ahead, and no sign of the mist clearing. The fifth milestone turned out to be only the fourth — still fifteen miles to Ludlow though it was much further over the hills — and when a man in a van stopped and offered me a lift I got in without a qualm. He didn't like to see anybody walking, he said, and he took me to Cleobury North. I asked him about a pub I had passed that was being enlarged and given a car park for about a hundred cars, and he said that although there was no village near it a rich man had bought it and was turning it into a super road-house, with no thought of expense.

"Easy come, easy go, I says," he said, and set me on the little road up to the Brown Clee. It took me steeply up into the mist. A squashed hedgehog lay in the road, and a dead cat in the hedge; there was silence save for the panting of my own breath and the ticking of an electric fence. Then I left the road and went further up into the woods, deeper into the mist.

I am not a countryman and I often wish I knew more about the things I see in the countryside. It would be nice to recognise wild flowers and rare trees and bird calls. I know a woodpecker when I see one, and a foxglove and a weasel and an ash-tree, but not much more. I picked a little red flower, probably one of the commonest autumn flowers in England, and put it in my button-hole, but I didn't know what it was. I expected, and hoped, to see a fox, or a badger, or even, in the mysterious fir plantation I walked through, something more mediaeval like a wolf or a small bear. But the dead hedgehog was the only wild animal I saw all day.

Nevertheless, though I might have appreciated more with more knowledge, and though it never became the glorious autumn day I had hoped for, it was all very beautiful, and the mist made it eerie and fantastic too. Full-rigged ships loomed out of the mist and turned into oak-trees, and a cock pheasant rose from the undergrowth in a tremendous flap and struggled up through the branches, scattering raindrops; it was like some prehistoric thing left from a million years ago. Huge golden chestnut leaves hung in suspense, or flopped gently to the ground, and everywhere was the sweet smell of decomposition. Best of all, everything was mine; there was nobody for miles, nobody else in the world.

I came out at the top of the wood, and walked on up through grazing sheep. Then I came to the first ramparts of Abdon Burf, a murky Iron Age fortress hovering in the mist. It was a legendary scene, Wagnerian and ritualistic, with ruined stone buildings standing in the middle — buildings erected for a strange purpose on an unrecognisable plan, with pits and wooden beams and the rusting bones of old machinery; men had once worked there, but I had no idea what they had done. I followed a track further up, curling through the mist to a padlocked hut with a dim pair of wireless masts. I was the highest man in Shropshire, with a view on a clear day across the borders of eight other counties, but I could hardly see a hundred yards.

I took another way down, past a deep lake — a flooded mine or a quarry or a volcano, but I couldn't see the other side — and headed due south, or so I thought. I congratulated myself on being able to read a map, cursed myself for not having brought a compass, comforted myself that I had never yet got lost on a mountain; and suddenly I came on the track leading back to the top. I had gone full circle and I laughed aloud, and a frightened sheep bucked in the grass and leapt into the mist.

Following sheep tracks over hummocks, through bogs and reeds and bracken, I found the woods again, and then a park railing and a road, which took me to a pub, and a pint of beer and cheese and chocolate.

I was back on the Ludlow road, but there was still another Clee ahead — Titterstone Clee — if I felt like it. I didn't really, but the beer bemused me and I took a side-road and then a muddy lane with rooks perched in the empty trees. Imperceptibly, between one Clee and the other, it seemed to have changed from autumn to winter. A dog barked at me as I left the lane and followed a path over open grazing that would take me across the shoulder of the hill, avoiding the top. Soon the path split into fragments and I picked the wrong one, which burrowed into a mass of bracken and never came out on the other side. Faintly I heard the sound of men's voices and machinery from above me; perhaps on Titterstone Clee they were still doing the same work that had once been done on Brown Clee; or perhaps there was nobody there at all. Eventually I reached a steep grass ramp with a rusty iron cable running down it, which took me to the cottages of Bedlam; there were rows of them, identical in red brick and lace curtains, but not a human being in sight, though I thought I heard the sound of a wireless. I walked on down, out of the mist, to Bitterley, where an old cottager and his wife were picking damsons. It began to rain and I had walked over twenty miles, so when a farmer offered to take me the remaining three miles into Ludlow I gratefully accepted.

*　　　*　　　*

I met the same farmer again next day in the Ludlow cattle market, where he had come to sell fifty mixed lambs. He was shuffling up and down in the rain between the pens, tossing up whether or not to bid for them himself, to drive the price up; but a neighbour of his had got caught out the week before and found himself buying his own sheep.

It was the rain and the cold that kept me another day in Ludlow, though there was nothing to be sorry about, for it must be one of the prettiest towns in England. Even if it wasn't for the hill and the castle and the River Teme curling round the town, there would be enough to commend it in the quantity of handsome houses, half-timbered of the seventeenth century and red brick of the eighteenth. And as at Bridgnorth there were shops full of things I wanted to have; it was all I could do to stop myself buying a pound of red Shropshire steak, and a fat cauliflower, and a wicker basket, and a besom, and a mahogany chest.

It was the same at the cattle market. Auctions mesmerise me; I find myself ineluctably catching the auctioneer's eye, half hoping that he will recognise me as a bidder, half terrified that I shall get landed with some extravagant item that I don't want and can't afford. It is the risk that is so intoxicating, and the fear not so much that the least wince or twitch may be mistaken for a bid, as that I shall lose my head and join in seriously. And what would I do with twelve bullocks?

The needle of the dial of a huge weighing-machine flicked erratically as bullocks and heifers were driven in batches into a covered ring—a sort of dung-strewn cockpit with the rain clattering on the tin roof—and stood huddled together and snorting in terror while men with sticks prodded their flanks and smacked their snouts. The auctioneer, in a little box in the corner like Mr Punch, began to scream; and the farmers, standing in tiers round the ring and looking faintly like the cattle, did nothing at all. One or two of them, of course, must have been doing something, because the bidding went up, but it was difficult not to believe that the whole thing was a conspiracy between the auctioneer and the men with sticks. The farmers made no sound and no move, except to light their pipes and cigarettes or occasionally to make a note on their catalogues.

The atmosphere was like that of a tyrannical court-room into which the cattle were driven for a summary trial; the judge-auctioneer had to get through as many cases as possible that afternoon, and the jurymen-farmers were required only to nod their assent before the prisoners were herded out into the rain—to execution or to a temporary reprieve, but in either case there were to be hours of further confinement in the pens and a miserable journey in a crowded truck, a bovine Black Maria. Sometimes they were driven out of the ring even before their case was finished, and the auctioneer had not yet banged down his mallet when the iron gates clanged behind them and another batch was driven in. For a horrified hour I watched beef being sold on the hoof for an average of one-and-threepence a pound, and quite apart from my normal weakness at auctions I felt an almost irresistible desire to buy a batch of cattle simply for the pleasure of setting them free.

Somehow I got away, and next morning I started on the wettest walk I have ever taken. The weather forecast promised an improvement, and I believed it. I took a bus from Ludlow up the valley of the River Onny, past Stokesay Castle and Craven Arms; where the bus continued over the hills to Church Stretton I got out and walked another four miles up the valley westwards, towards Wales and into the rain. Cars splashed past me, their windows tight shut and their wipers busy on the windscreen;

occasionally a face looked out, pale and dry and sardonic. A heron flew down the valley over my head, going the other way, back towards Ludlow.

At the southern end of the Long Mynd I left the road and began to climb. The Long Mynd is a great moorland ridge, with an escarpment on the west, a series of deep valleys cutting into it on the east, a prehistoric track called the Port Way along the top, and a terrific view. But though the visibility was better than it had been two days earlier on the Clee Hills and I did sometimes get a glimpse of wet green fields below me, I had nothing of the treat I had hoped for; and it rained all day.

Three miles from the beginning, after meeting only a few wild horses and some grouse, I came to a group of buildings surrounded by caravans and strange covered trailers. "The centre of British gliding", said a notice, and I would have given a lot for a ride up above the rain in one of those marvellous long-winged planes. I walked round the club house and looked in through the windows. A family was having a picnic inside, and two young men were playing billiards; when they saw me they put down their cues and stared out at me in silence and in horror, which made me so uncomfortable that I went back to the Port Way and continued my walk. Another three miles further on, at Boiling Well, a signpost pointed down to Church Stretton. Weakly I turned off the Long Mynd and hurried down hill.

Rain, once one is drenched, ceases to be a question of degree, and it doesn't matter whether it is drizzling or pouring. In Church Stretton it was still raining, but I didn't notice, or care, how hard. It was probably the sight of the remains of a market in the square, with stacks of soggy blankets lying on a table, that decided me, though I think I had known for several hours that I wasn't going on with my plan for walking over the Shropshire hills. In the bus to Shrewsbury I emptied the water out of my shoes under the seat. At Shrewsbury station I bought a pair of socks and an evening paper, and in the lavatory at the station I dried my feet on the paper before putting on the socks. And at Paddington, as I had suspected all along, the clouds had gone and the sky was full of stars. Next morning in London it was soft and warm and golden again.

VI

BRIDGWATER

SATURDAY was wedding-day in Bridgwater, all over the town, and as the peals tumbled from the belfries and the photographers adjusted the bridal drapes, the guests turned thirstily to celebration. There were more than a hundred of them, with a jazz band, in the pub where I stayed; and long after the couple had been seen off to their honeymoon, long after the bridesmaids, pressing wilted bouquets in sticky fingers to tulle bodices, had been taken home, long after most people could remember who it was who got married, the drinking went on.

Slowly it merged into the normal business of Saturday night. The drums were piled up in the passage behind the bar, the drifts of confetti disappeared like melting snow, keg bitter was poured in on top of Dry Monopole, and the men with white carnations trooping to the lavatory were lost among the men without them.

In another pub down the street a middle-aged couple was hopping among the tables, while a man punched away at a husky piano. 'Somebody stole my girl', they all sang, and the darts were flying wild. When a pint glass crashed to the ground the pianist switched into 'Marching through Georgia'. A pearly-coloured woman with a bronchial cough, ageless and rather tight, came in; she had been to the pictures, *Tom Jones*, which was partly filmed in Bridgwater, but nothing had impressed her except the actresses: "They've got wonderful bosoms on them, right up here," and she demonstrated with her own.

"All right, Cis," said a man in the corner, with an eye on me, the stranger in Bridgwater, "I've got a pair at home." But she was incorrigible, and went on about her pins and needles and her palpitations, until somebody bought her a drink.

Sunday was driving-lesson day, and while the pupils battled through the streets, with their engines either stalled or racing, the loafers ogled from the pavement in the hope of a collision, too intent even for a glance at a ravishing Salvation Army girl tripping to a meeting in black nylons and patent leather stilettos. A few old Austins brought a few old Christians to matins at Saint Mary's; and under the tower which the Duke of Monmouth, king of a fortnight, climbed to survey his uncle's troops camped on Sedgemoor, a young clergyman quoted Julian Huxley to a congregation of ladies in navy blue straw hats and gentlemen in shiny grey Burton suits. "Man is a puny thing living on a planet spinning like a dirty tennis ball," he told them, and the people who might have listened were spinning along the road to Weston-super-Mare.

At first it all seemed familiar; there was nothing strange about Bridgwater, unlike Blyth and Leek. In Blyth, a working-class town, the mayor had been a coal-miner, and in Leek, a textile town, he had worn wooden clogs, but in Bridgwater, a town of supreme normality, he was the personnel manager of the biggest factory; nothing very exotic about that. Bridgwater wasn't way out, as the others had been; the process of emancipation and national standardisation had gone further, and even the people's conversation suggested a reluctance to betray any oddities, as though a phenomenon would be an embarrassment. Men in pubs hailed each other with "Long time no see", they asked each other where they stayed when they went to London, they reckoned that the Noël Coward play they saw in town last week had dated a bit, they went out to stroke the immense Jaguar the landlord kept in the back yard, and they finished their drinks and said, "Cheerio, old boy, all the best." It might have been Beaconsfield or Bromley as much as Bridgwater.

For that reason it was not surprising to find so many restaurants —Fish, Steak, Parisian, Chinese, Continental, Trust House. Chips with everything, of course, whether veal escalope or sweet and sour pork, but nothing was quite so dismal as the chips that went with a great rocky lump enclosing a small grey substance that had once, in a distant life, swum in the sea; all memory of that life was smothered by oil and a protective casing of batter; and Bridgwater, to make it sadder, was a seaport.

But there were surprises, all the same, though they struck surreptitiously. One of the first was Bridgwater's proud history, with Admiral Blake standing on the Cornhill directing the traffic, and three miles away at Weston Zoyland—a village with a written-in Somerset burr—a painted notice pointing 'to the battlefield' with such immediacy as though to say that if one hurried the dead might still be warm and the blood not yet congealed. Judge Jeffreys was well forgotten, but over the site where a royalist castle for weeks defied the Cromwellian sympathies of the population there was now one of the most beautiful eighteenth-century streets in England; and in that street, for a town that is neither a university nor a cathedral town nor even the county town of Somerset, was the biggest surprise of all — the Arts Centre.

In a country where the oldest something-or-other is itself a claim to importance, Bridgwater has two trumps; it is the borough with the oldest charter in Somerset, granted in 1200, and it has the oldest Arts Centre in England, founded in 1946. Complete with its own little theatre, with advertisements for the next visit of the Bournemouth Symphony Orchestra and with morning coffee for the ladies, the Arts Centre is the hot-bed of Bridgwater culture; and round it revolve no less than three drama groups, societies devoted to opera, music, choral singing, films, history and literary discussions, and the Bridgwater Youth Orchestra.

For anyone who boggles at such high-brow stuff, there are milder, more homespun things. Further into the cultural outback hover the members of societies for pantomime, variety, flower arrangement, ballroom-dancing and stamp-collecting; and far beyond the reach of the Arts Centre, in a jungle of philistinism, flit the votaries of bee-keeping, body-building, chrysanthemum-growing, budgerigar-breeding, and every sport from skittles to euchre. It is wonderful how diligently the people of Bridgwater will look for an excuse to form a society; they have special ones for Welshmen, Rationalists, Industrial Christians, Polish Combatants, Allotment Holders, World Friends, Mid-Somerset Aquarists, Women Electricians, Head Teachers, Friends of Spastics, and Afternoon Townswomen — all these, and a hundred and fifty more, in a town of twenty-five thousand people.

"It is a market town turning industrial," said the town clerk, and I remembered his words when I saw a woman in the street with a vegetable marrow in one hand and a violin case in the other. I was getting used to Bridgwater's little secrets, and I wasn't surprised even at learning that it is the official twin town of the Mediterranean port of La Ciotat, a relationship conceived under the family plan of the Movement for a Bilingual World.

The town clerk, whose father had been town clerk of Blyth and who had spent most of his early life in the north of England, talked about the fleshpots of the south, and said he wouldn't go back now for anything. At first he had been a little put off, after the straightforward behaviour of northerners, by the devious methods of these Somerset folk, and he complained that they would never really say what they thought — or at least not until they had already begun to think something else. His wife, too, had been irritated by the slowness of Bridgwater life; when she went into a shop she had been treated to a long conversation before being served, not out of thoughtlessness but simply because these people worked in a different way. But they had both been won over, if not by the gentle climate and the social tranquillity, then by the local dramatics and the visiting string quartets.

To me the only jarring note in such a genial town was the notice, stuck in the window of almost every pub, "No gipsies served here." It showed a vehemence quite out of character, and nobody could really explain the reason. "The gipsies, you see," one man told me cryptically, "come down from the Quantocks," as though that explained it all; while another man said, "The gipsies, you see, come down from the Mendips." A third said, "They come for the pea-picking," and a fourth said, more plausibly, "They get a skinful of cider."

*   *   *

The town clerk's description, "a market town turning industrial", is almost too modest for a place that makes a variety of things from beer and jam to shoes and brassières; the old industries of tiles and basket furniture, though they still exist, have slowly given way to cellophane packings and electronic equipment, and nobody seems to know whether Bath bricks, once made on the banks of the River Parrett and used by generations of sailors for polishing battleships, are still produced. It is a revolution that has obliterated the unemployment of thirty years ago and brought brash new factories to the marshy waste lands up and down the Parrett.

The Parrett, which is the reason for Bridgwater's existence, also accounts for its limitations. It is a twisting, muddy river only navigable at high tide and not at all at neaps. That was all very well in the days of small sailing vessels, and photographs taken a hundred years ago, and even at the turn of the century, show schooners and brigantines moored thickly right up to the iron bridge in the middle of the town. But in a similar position up another river not far along the coast is the port of Bristol, twenty times the size of Bridgwater, and the difference is a source of contention. Bristol, say the cynics, would never have prospered without the slave trade, whereas Bridgwater was actually the first town to petition Parliament for its abolition. Bridgwater, others say, was cut off from the rest of the country by the swamps and peat bogs of Sedgemoor, while Bristol was more accessible to the midlands. But the truth is the simple fact that the Avon is a much better river than the Parrett.

In Bridgwater tall brick warehouses still stand among the Georgian houses along West Quay, and a notice on the town bridge records the times and height of the tidal bore that comes up the Parrett twice a day; but weeds grow between the stones where ships were moored, and it is a long time since a warp was last thrown round any of the rusting iron bollards. On the other bank rotting wharfs are falling into the mud, and despite a faded notice on a warehouse advertising "Regular steamers between Bridgwater and Bristol Channel ports" it is all too obvious that the last steamer sailed away long ago, and in fact the firm now runs lorries.

There is only one shipping agent left, in an office with a mercury barometer on the wall outside that hasn't been tapped for years, and an old clock inside ticking away among the clearance papers and bills of lading. A clerk stands up at a high desk, and an old man says, "I remember when I was a boy . . ." so that one can almost see the pattern of masts and rigging through his window-panes.

But despite the deserted quays along the Parrett the old agent still has plenty of work, for the shipping tonnage passing through Bridgwater is actually greater now than it was fifty years ago, even if the number of ships has declined. Round the bend of the river is a dock basin, originally built for the canal that runs up to Taunton, and although the canal is now clogged with duckweed and unused except by anglers, in the basin there is usually a collier from South Wales, and a small German coaster with a cargo of wood pulp or cattle feed, and a timber boat from some improbable Dutch port. The dock is owned by British Railways, and it makes no profit for them; but, as the mayor said, would it be sad if the port of Bridgwater were to close down, though he admitted that the borough itself could never afford to run it.

Nostalgia, however, is not one of Bridgwater's strong points. In the last few years acres of old buildings, criss-crossed by narrow streets, have been razed in the cause of slum clearance and traffic relief. 'Sub-standard' is the official word for the pretty houses that have been felled, and it is hard to imagine just what—and whose—the standard is. "That's all coming down," said the mayor with relish, about some nice old brick buildings; and when I protested that they looked all right to me, he said that it was like an old man's teeth, and that the front ones may look good enough but the back ones were shockers.

But it is too easy to exaggerate the picture of the city fathers slavering happily at the thought of still more old streets to demolish; for in fact they have a plan for the centre of the town which, so far from destroying the character and prosperity of the place as some people fear, will probably restore its former peacefulness. By building ring-roads and car-parks, and by making new streets for tradesmen's vans at the back of the shops, they hope to be able to cut the main shopping streets off from traffic and reserve them for pedestrians only. It seems a fine idea, which only the shopkeepers in the town centre oppose, and there is now a battle between the planners, who have not yet finished their plan and say that anyway it will take thirty years to implement, and the *status quo*-ists, who have no idea how else to deal with the traffic. A visitor too suffers a similar conflict, between the inner conservative in him and the inner radical.

There is one man, however, who takes no part in the fray. He is not a Bridgwater man, but a Londoner, an old bachelor with a white beard who lives there in retirement. He sits in a big room above the Oddfellows' Hall on West Quay, with a grandfather clock and his books in mahogany shelves and his mother's willow pattern tea service, chain-smoking cigarettes and looking through his window at the deserted Parrett. Once he was the editor of a scientific journal and wrote a learned book on his subject, but now, though he still gets sent the journal, he has lost interest in it; besides, as he says, it is so advanced that he can't understand it any more. Instead, he burrows in the Bridgwater archives, shuttles between the public library and the Arts Centre, and arranges his albums of photographs. By patiently waiting for the season, or the sun, or the traffic, he has assembled a collection of pictures of every notable building in Bridgwater—just as fine as the collection that another photographer made a hundred years ago and which is now in the museum. In a few years his own pictures will be an equally valuable record of how the town once appeared; and many of the buildings in them have already gone. Whenever another church or pub is handed over to the demolishers the old scientist, desperately and lovingly but quite un-bitterly, takes his camera out for a last picture—only just in time, sometimes, and he showed me a shot of a bakery that he had watched being knocked down by a bull-dozer; it took just ten minutes to smash a building in which a family of bakers had made bread for centuries.

Meanwhile, as Bridgwater struggles with its growing pains, there are the inevitable anachronisms. Within sight of the chimney of the town's biggest factory I watched a farmer sitting in a field milking his cows into a bucket; and in the town hall one night several hundred teen-agers twisted in the dark, while in a pub next door their grandfathers filled themselves with rough draught cider.

"In my young day, if I wanted to put my arm round a girl, I didn't have to go to a dance to do it," said a toothless fellow of sixty-two, gulping at his eighth pint and lamenting the decline of cider drinking. He himself had left home at fourteen to work on a farm on Sedgemoor; in those days he would get up at five in the morning, drink a pint of cider before milking the cows, drink more at breakfast and more again at dinner; the first cup of tea of the day was at supper, when he came in from work, and the evening was given up to cider. One night, for a bet, he had drunk fourteen pints in an hour and a half, and then bicycled three miles home. But he was a connoisseur of cider; he used to make his own and prime it with raw meat; he would put a big joint of beef in the vat on Friday night, and by Sunday morning the meat would be dissolved and he could pull the bone out clean. There was no cider quite like his.

*   *   *

Bridgwater was deceptive, and I found that more of old Somerset survived than I at first suspected; at no time was it so concentrated as on the opening day of the Saint Matthew's Fair. For the three succeeding days the town surrendered to the extortion of showmen who had been doing the same at Barnstaple the week before and would be doing it again at the Nottingham Goose Fair a week later; but on the first day, for the sheep and horse sales that were the original point of the fair, the bumpkins of all Somerset came to Saint Matthew's Field. The modern world was forgotten in the brewery marquee and the surrounding pubs, and the Somerset burr hung in the air as thick as the smell of sheep.

Fine men with purple faces, in corduroy trousers, wellingtons, check jackets and tweed caps, leaned over hurdles and poked into the sheep's wool with their sticks, grunting in the way their ancestors had done. The bidding was as slow as only Somerset men could make it, and a brisk auctioneer had a hard time to get through five thousand sheep in the morning. Too often a farmer buying ewes would hold up everything for a long, hard look into their teeth; and too often a farmer selling ram lambs would watch the price stop at twenty guineas and then withdraw and take them all home again.

More lively was the horse-coping at the other end of the field, where Exmoor ponies, donkeys and goats were being offered by quick-witted men impatient to clinch a sale. And beyond the fairground in a street closed to traffic, full-throated hucksters with a bewildering patter of plausibility and obscenity were selling off bargains — non-stick saucepans, meretricious tea-sets, Christine Keeler pillow-cases and real Italian bed-sheets with real Italian directions for use — to housewives from every village between Bristol and Bideford, while their husbands struggled into five-bob jackets and haggled over army surplus boots. Jews and Indians and Africans and Arabs had come to the Saint Matthew's Fair, and also gipsies, but they alone, for their elusive local reputation, were not allowed inside the bulging beer-tent.

The fair-ground itself, after the sheep sales were over, showed up the behaviour of several hundred Somerset farmers turned loose among a handful of showmen out for their money. Of course a diet of hot dogs, toffee apples and candy floss can wreck the most stubborn of bucolic principles, as can the knowledge that the wife and daughter and mother-in-law are rooted to the bingo tables; but it might be thought that for these yokels an exhibition offering a pig with two bodies, a ram with five legs, and a hen with three feet would be irresistible. Not at all. The dodgems and the wall of death were left, understandably, to the youngsters; a loud-speaker van from some non-denominational mission was hurried past in silence, the old coconut shies and try-your-strength machines were hardly more popular, and the hoop-las and rifle ranges, and even a tent that promised the juiciest wrestling and the rawest boxing in the land, were almost abandoned. What these farmers, from the Mendips and the Poldens and the Quantocks, from Sedgemoor and Taunton Deane, from the edge of the Cots-wolds and the Blackdowns and the frontiers of Dorset and Devon —what they wanted, simply, was nudes.

On a floodlit platform in front of a tent three girls in bikinis, with golden tassels swinging from the points of their brassières, wiggled to the blare of a radiogram, and below them stood a gasping, goggle-eyed crowd of Somerset men, their hands in their pockets and their boots gently rocking in the mud. When the crowd was big enough, the girls went into the tent; the men, slily grinning, followed them in, and for a shilling watched them take their bikinis off.

For myself, a shilling was better spent in a tent ignored by the farmers. In it I found myself standing alone and talking to an almost naked girl, about six inches high, squatting inside a gold-fish bowl. She came, she told me, from British Colombia, and when I asked her how she liked being in a goldfish bowl, she said it was all right for a laugh; besides, she added, it gave her a chance of seeing England. It was an odd encounter, even for Bridgwater.

Perhaps, on the other hand, one should not be surprised at Bridgwater. The girl in the goldfish bowl may be unique, but there must be plenty of other towns in the south of England which once flourished as ports or corn markets or centres of manufacturing or cloth-milling, and which lost their trade to other parts of England and never found a substitute. At first they lapsed into a gentle decline, but now, if they are like Bridgwater, they are strenuously making up for lost time. For a visitor it is easy to be nostalgic, particularly if one has a liking for a town's individuality, let alone a taste for decay. For the people who live there, however, it is probably the most important, and the most exciting, epoch of their history.

*   *   *

Once a year, for a few hours after dark one day in early November, Bridgwater goes mad. They call it the Guy Fawkes Carnival, but the fact that it doesn't happen on November the fifth unless that is early closing day doesn't worry anybody, because any connection with the Gunpowder Plot is long forgotten. They don't even have a bonfire on the Cornhill nowadays, but they do still celebrate the ancient custom of squibbing.

"Carnival be buggered," said a man in the Golden Ball, buying himself a pint of beer and half a bottle of Scotch whisky. "I'm going to sit down in an armchair with my bottle of Scotch, open a book and turn on the telly. Maybe I'll go to sleep. Maybe the book and the telly won't get much attention. But the Scotch will. I'll be as happy as a sandboy. All I want is a blonde."

"The wife away then?" asked another man.

"Only for the afternoon. Gone to Bristol. She'll be back tonight. Wish she'd go away for a fortnight again." Then, after a gulp at his beer, he added, "I've only just got over the last one." The carnival or the wife — there was no telling.

All afternoon, after the shops had shut, men worked in the High Street, getting it ready for the riot. Everywhere there was a feeling of imminent disaster, as if bad news had reached the town; the buildings were going to be demolished by an earthquake, or the enemy had crossed the Parrett; the Duke of Monmouth would have recognised the situation. The town hall was battened down to withstand the worst, windows were boarded up, shops were encased in timber and canvas, the pubs were cleared of furniture, Admiral Blake was wrapped up in a tarpaulin jacket, carpenters took over the pavements, and I got a chunk of sawdust in my eye and had to go to hospital to have it removed.

At dusk little droves of special constables began to collect at street corners, like carrion crows. 'No Bore Today' read the notice on the town bridge over the Parrett, as though even nature had been asked to stay away. Instead, a lorry drove in from the north with four earnest young men in the cab and 'Fun is our Business' painted on the front.

"Bridgwater Carnival's the biggest in the country," said a grey old man weaving wicker baskets down by the river. "But it's not what it was. They used to run special trains from Bristol and South Wales and even London. They had the bonfire on the

Cornhill, in front of Admiral Blake there, until they put down that tarmac and it all melted. Sticky for days, it was."

I had seen his cottage light on and looked through the window. He was sitting among a pile of basket chairs and tables making a strange and pretty little object, a twisted cage on a stalk, and when he saw me watching him he beckoned me in. It was a baby's rattle, he said, dropping a silver bell into it, tying the ends together and giving it to me. "You can have it for four-and-six." Years ago a lady had brought one to him, an old thing she had found in a museum somewhere, and asked him to copy it. He couldn't take it to pieces, but sat looking at it for hours, figuring out how to make it.

"You would never have seen how to do it," he said, but not unkindly. He took up five willow osiers from the floor, and bound them together; then, twisting and tucking and pulling, he conjured another little cage between his knees.

"You could never do it," he said, popping the bell in and finishing off the ends. "The knot at the end—that's where you'd be stumped."

In self-defence I picked up one of his tools, to show I knew what it was. "That's a marline-spike," I said.

"That's what some people call it, but it isn't." In ten minutes he had finished the second rattle, and I bought it too. You wouldn't get the young people now to make things like that, the old man said, but without regret. He didn't blame them; there was no future in basket-weaving, but he felt no nostalgia and he had no desire to see his trade perpetuated; perhaps he was proud to be the only man still at it, the last of a race. When his daughter came in and said that tea was ready, he came to the door to see me off and look at the weather. "Should be a fine night for the carnival. I hope so, for the sake of the boys. They put a lot of hours into it."

The Bridgwater Spectacular began with a whimper. I stood in the crowd on the town bridge and watched a procession led by two fire engines creep past. Immense floats with tableaux entitled 'There was an old woman who lived in a shoe' or 'The wedding of Lorna Doone' were punctuated by the display lorries of commercial firms, cars from driving schools and a fishmonger's van loaded with kippers and fillets of plaice. After about two hours the last float, 'The Willow Pattern', rolled on to the bridge. No bore today, indeed.

"You should see a real carnival, man," said a West Indian as an earnest person in a raincoat slipped out of the crowd, hoisted a board — 'Eternity, Heaven or Hell?' — above his head and followed the procession up the street. But Bridgwater had done its duty, and now it gave itself up to squibbing. The High Street became a crazy, screaming, terrifying trap of bangs and flashes. Young men walking down the street idly dropped bangers behind the most vulnerable girls; rockets were set off from the litter baskets on the lamp-posts; nylon stockings were laddered; a fire engine clanged through the crowd; something flashed through my hair and exploded inside the public bar of the Golden Ball; a schoolmaster with scorched trousers said, "All right, Briggs, see you on Monday," and a deaf man asked me, "When's the squibbing?"

At about ten o'clock sixty men marched down the High Street, pushing aside the crowd and each carrying a monstrous firework tied to a pole. They lined up in front of the town hall and a man blew a whistle. Somebody put a match to a rag of paraffin and the men put their fuses to the flame. Then they stood up, holding the poles above their heads. There was a great hissing noise, and showers of gold spurted up from the fireworks and rained down on the crowd. It was marvellous. For five minutes the High Street was drenched in a glory of golden rain, a street of burning effervescence. Then, with a final whoomph! sixty immense fireworks, one after another, exploded and sent a last cascade of liquid gold high over the rooftops. The men staggered under the force.

"They're about fifteen bob each," said a huge Somerset policeman standing impassively beside me. And half an hour later the High Street was empty.

VII

SWANAGE

AFTER Guy Fawkes' Day, when Remembrance Day follows and
the sun sets at four-thirty in the afternoon, autumn slips quietly
off the calendar and only the weather can put off winter for another
week. In those twilight days between the seasons, with drifts of
leaves bowling along the roads, with the sun shining through the
rain and rainbows arched across the sky, with a touch of morning
frost on the roof slates and a momentary chill in the beer, with a
new Prime Minister fighting in Scotland to get elected to Parliament and a crucial by-election being held at Luton, with the
decorations going up in Oxford Street and the first Father
Christmas striking his annual shudder in my bones, I escaped to a
town where 'the season' means only a giddy month or two of
English summer, and the rest is silence.

I went to Swanage. Other people had gone there too, but not
many. There were a few elderly ladies dressed as holiday-makers
sitting in a shelter on the seafront, writing Mabel Lucie Attwell
postcards to their friends; there was a little black boy dressed as a
Red Indian playing alone with a scarlet plastic bucket in a corner
of the beach; there were stalwarts dressed as yachtsmen standing
in a pub round a girl in turned-down sea-boots; there was a brave
woman in an old-fashioned bathing-suit splashing into the sea
when the rain stopped; and there was a storm-beaten old salt
dressed as a lifeboatman, but a little too good to be true, as though
he had been sent down from London to pose for a travel poster
and the storm-beating had been painted on by a make-up man.

Otherwise the town was left to the caretakers, waiting for next
Easter or Whitsun or August, and hoping that they would do
better than they had last year. Most of the hotels and cafés were
shut, together with the photo kiosks and super dodgems. Even
the seagulls had disappeared, perhaps across the bay to Bournemouth, and it was almost a surprise that the breakers still rolled
on the sand and the water still flushed in the public lavatories; in

78

fact, with the only decent restaurant closing down at eight-fifteen and nothing to be had after that but fish and chips, the public lavatories, more numerous than in any other town I know, were the only places that offered full service out of season. But the soiled gaiety of a seaside town caught early in its hibernation and not yet tarnished by the winter months was a phenomenon peculiar to an elusive English season, and made Swanage an appropriate setting for a November weekend.

The caretakers, in tweed caps if they were male and plastic hairbags if female, exercised their dogs along the sand and went to meetings of the Ladies' Circle, the Inner Wheel or the Rotary. Some of them were professionals who had been in the seaside business all their lives, but many of them were retired people marooned in Swanage by the comparative failure of their careers and for whom the lights of Bournemouth flickering across the sea represented the golden pensioned years that might have been; a bigger push in youth, a more perceptive boss, a little extra luck — and another promotion before retiring — would have made Bournemouth more than just a monthly trip and a ritual argument over whether to go to *Lilac Time* or the Winter Gardens. As it was, in Swanage, there was only Friday bingo and the empty, padlocked months before the lights went up again.

However there was one alternative — Miss Gem Lloyd's season of plays old and new in the little hall at the end of the seafront — though only twenty-six people turned up the night I went. Some of them were done up in overcoats and ear-rings, and most of them seemed to treat the show as a bit of a joke.

"Aren't you in it tonight?" a woman asked the programme girl.

"Not till after the interval."

"How long's the interval?"

"As long as it take us to change the set." She wore tight black trousers and a lively green man's shirt; the breast pocket sagged with the pennies she collected for the programmes. It was a double bill of one-act plays by Tennessee Williams and Strindberg, and perhaps not so surprising that the Swanage people stayed away.

"I live at Parkstone really," said a rimless woman with a blue rinse on her head and four eternity rings on her fingers; she didn't want to be taken for a Swanage resident. "My daughter's just gone off to California. It was such a job getting her away. So I came here for a week's holiday, to get over it all." I met her in a hotel made up of three Victorian villas joined together, with fitted carpets and a fat Welsh corgi sitting in the bar.

"I always think the Queen's corgis look so—so sporting," said a chattery widow who lived in a bungalow on the hill with her sister. Suddenly she recognised a young man at the bar and dashed over to him: "You don't remember me, I'm sure"—and weakly he blushed and waited for her to explain.

"Are you going up to the Boat Show this year, Michael?" he asked his companion when the widow had left.

There were old men who had once ruled an empire, who spoke impeccable Swahili and Pushtu and Cantonese, who had built railways, levied taxes and sentenced the natives to death. Here they were, in a Swanage hotel with their deaf-aids and their shabby suits, waiting for somebody to finish with the *Illustrated London News*.

"Harold dear, do you remember those nice people we met on the boat to Singapore?"

There were young, post-imperial families on leave from the tropics—the husbands, sunburnt and impatient, fixing up games of squash, and the wives, pretty in pearls and cardigans, trying to cope with their children in the hotel dining-room.

"I simply can't wait to have an amah again."

"The number of people in the parish who only put sixpence in the collection!" snorted a churchwarden, a retired naval officer. "It's disgusting. D'you realise, sixpence keeps us going for precisely three and a half minutes?"

There were parents with their sons out from one of the preparatory schools for the half-term holiday. They looked so bored, both parents and sons; they hadn't seen each other for six weeks, but they had nothing at all to say.

Swanage is a town of prep schools, run by pink-faced men in check jackets and striped ties. I had been at one of them myself, for two years before the war, leaving at the end of that queer summer of 1939, and this time I went back to see what it was like. It was a journey back to 1939 too, and to childhood, and to thoughts and hopes and dreads that had escaped me for twenty-four years. On the way I passed another school, against which we had played cricket matches, but it had been turned into a convalescent home for Warwickshire coal-miners; it was probably doing a better job now, I felt, and partly from terror and partly from a feeling that private prep schools are a modern anachronism, I began to hope that my old school too had been converted into something else. But it hadn't, and I walked up the drive in a mood of alarm.

"Awfully nice of you to come," said the headmaster. "Twenty-four years, is it really? Extraordinary. Doesn't seem a day." To me it seemed exactly twenty-four years. "I expect you'll see a lot of changes in the place." And to me it seemed exactly, terrifyingly the same. In the classrooms were the same old lockers, the same desks with carved initials, the same dry smell of chalk dust, the same view — for an inattentive boy — of stone buildings through diagonal window panes. Only the dark green paint that had covered everything in my time was missing, and the boys, instead of wearing grey tweed knickerbockers as we had, were now in corduroy shorts.

"Got rid of those dreadful things years ago," said the head-master. "So insanitary, apart from anything else." He had also got rid of the Latin master who smelt of whisky, and the curious mud battles we used to have down in the woods when it was too wet for football, and the run over the hills on summer mornings to bathe naked in the sea from the rocks at Dancing Ledge. We walked across the grounds and met a boy holding a transistor radio to his ear.

"The London Counties match, what?" said the headmaster. "What's the score?"

"Eight nil, sir," piped the boy. "It's a slaughter."

The changing-room was the most powerful evocation: the odour of football clothes hanging on pegs, the mud trodden into the wooden floor, the playboxes containing precious things sent from home, the misery of hours wasted on a cricket field. So much came back, and there was so much I wanted to ask, but didn't; Do the boys still have to write a letter home before church on Sunday mornings, and leave it unsealed on a table in the head-master's hall, so that he can inspect it before the post goes? Does the cocoa still leave a film of grit inside one's mouth? Do the boys still collect in the lavatory round a boy who has been beaten, to inspect his stripes? And there was something I wanted to say, but didn't either: That I had never liked the place very much, but now I hated it.

*   *   *

On Remembrance Sunday afternoon the British Legion procession began on the seafront, between a poster recommending
holidays in Nice and an obelisk commemorating a naval battle
fought by Alfred the Great in Swanage Bay against the Danes.
White-haired men with Pip, Squeak and Wilfred in their lapels
and grey-haired men with the Spam Medal and stern women in
overcoats labelled 'Welfare' or 'Commandant' collected on the
pavement. There were also policemen, firemen, bandsmen, terri-
torials, reservists, and all sorts of citizens in uniform, wearing
poppies and carrying wreaths. They saluted each other, hesitantly
and clumsily at first, but more boldly as they got back into
practice. A furtive nun slipped across the road in front of the
paraders, but nobody noticed her.

The band led the way through the empty town to the parish
church; there it unbuckled its instruments and filed into its place
in the north transept. The church was already full, and hardly had
the marchers got their breath back than they were on their feet
again, praising, their souls, the King of Heaven. 'Ransomed,
healed, restored, forgiven' — but for what? It was hard to remember. Salerno was twenty years ago, the Somme forty-five. There
had once been sand and mud, there had been Lili Marlene and
Mad'm'zelle from Armentières, there had been whale meat and
plum-and-apple, and somewhere there had even been poppies. But
here, with the little mayor fingering his chain and his petty officer's
cap on the pew beside him ('Praise Him for His grace and favour'),
with the town dignitaries laying their wreaths and banners at the
altar ('Father-like He tends and spares us'), with the rector standing like a Victorian painting of the wrath of God ('Saints
triumphant, bow before Him') — here in the Swanage parish
church, so far from 1918 and in a paradoxical way so much further
from 1945, it was difficult to see the point of so much remembrance.

"He used to be chaplain at Sandringham," whispered the lady
next to me. "We're very proud of his red cassock."

"They shall grow not old," said a man in a round Dorset voice,
lighting a Toc H lamp, "as we that are left grow old." How many
people in the congregation, I wondered, could put a name to any
of the men he was talking about? "At the going down of the sun
and in the morning, we will remember them."

"We will remember them," echoed the rector and the mayor

and the naval churchwarden and the men in regimental ties and the women in uniform and the two little girls in front of me and the choirboys and the lady who was so proud of the link with Sandringham, reading the words on the printed order of service; but twenty minutes later, lining up in the road for the procession to the war memorial, we had already forgotten.

"Parade!" shouted a man, with the authority of someone who has once been an officer, but also with the diffidence of someone who hasn't been an officer for a long time; he had grown middle-aged in an England which stands to attention with reluctance, and perhaps he hardly believed we would obey him. But even after all these years it worked: "Parade" — and then that extraordinary English syllable that adds another inch to the height of full-grown men, pulls their chests out and drives their left feet smartly up to their right. By the right, we quick marched in tiny steps, perhaps for the sake of the women, back through the empty streets, past the public lavatories and up into the public recreation ground. There the officer's confidence began to fail, buffeted by the wind blowing up from the beach. "Right turn, please," he urged, on a dying cadence, and in time the procession was drawn up before the memorial, facing the sea in the darkening afternoon.

"John!" called the rector to the officer, in a panic. "John, what do we do now?" The wind was tearing at the cloak he had put on over his red Sandringham cassock, and he clearly was not going to linger over the ceremony. Hastily he took the wreaths from the curate, who took them from the men and women who marched up to the memorial, and propped them on the steps. Some of them were blown over by the wind. It was as perfunctory and inelegant as the ritual at a Hindu shrine. The children at the other end of the recreation ground went on playing on the swings, quite uncurious about the ceremony, and the lights of Bournemouth were switched on across the bay.

Then something — a reaction to the banality of the performance, or a sergeant of the Dorset Regiment who saluted with fervid defiance as he surrendered his wreath, or the maudlin vibrato of the trumpets in the Last Post, or the sloppy drilling of the standard-bearers as they dipped their banners for the national anthem, or perhaps a touch of private shame at my own irreverence — something suddenly brought a tear to my eye, a tear that I couldn't pretend was brought by the sea wind. Then, just as suddenly, it was all over. "Parade! Dis—" and almost before the "—miss!" was out the rector was hurrying away through the bathing huts to his car, and the Needles lighthouse was flashing over the sea from the Isle of Wight.

I left Swanage that evening and stopped in a village pub. There were pigs' tails and trotters in the bar, and a man playing shove-ha'penny who couldn't have been born yet in 1945. "Good thing Labour won at Luton," he said, rubbing the board with the palm of his hand, and already the remembrance service was as remote as the Flanders fields.

VIII

LOWESTOFT

"He even thinks like a herring," somebody said to me in Lowestoft. But although herrings constituted his thoughts and his dreams as well as most of his food, there was nothing of a herring in his appearance. Jumbo Fiske, skipper of the *Suffolk Warrior*, a Lowestoft herring drifter, was immense. Twenty-three stone, they said—not far short of a cran—and they also said that when the *Suffolk Warrior* was coming into harbour you could tell from ashore which side of the wheelhouse the skipper was standing on, by the list in her mast. What is certainly true is that when Jumbo was at the wheel there was no room to pass, and if you wanted to get from the port side of the wheelhouse to the starboard you had to go outside and walk round by the funnel. To hold the wheel, he stood with his feet about a yard away from it and leant forward so that his belly brushed the spokes. His belly, because of its amplitude, was where he kept his voice, which explained the magnificent diapason he commanded; and another curious thing about Jumbo Fiske was the soft pendulous dewlap sprinkled with white stubble that hung over the silk scarf he wore round his neck, below his huge potato face.

I first met Jumbo having breakfast down in the crew's mess of the *Suffolk Warrior*, eating a plateful of fresh herrings with his fingers; they looked like whitebait in his hands. He had just come in after two nights' fishing, with only five crans of herring—less than a ton—and the oaths, slipping from his belly as fast as the herrings went in, testified to his disgust. This was supposed to be the height of the East Anglican herring season, or the East Anglian voyage as they call it, and even at the inflated prices due to the bad catches he couldn't expect to get more than seventy-five pounds for his two nights' fishing; and it costs nearly six hundred pounds a week to keep a herring drifter running. One of the troubles—and there were plenty of them, from the gales that had made it sometimes impossible to shoot the nets, to the big fleets of foreign herring trawlers that had appeared in the North Sea in recent years—was the *Suffolk Warrior*'s capstan; this machine, for which Jumbo used his favourite four-letter word in a cascade of startling repetition, had broken down and the crew had had to haul in a mile or so of nets by hand, all for five crans of herring. It made you weep; and if you were Jumbo you wept not tears but another torrent of that little pudendal word.

Not that the *Suffolk Warrior* had done badly during the year. On the first Aberdeen voyage between April and June when the Lowestoft drifters sail from Scotland to the herring grounds off the Shetlands and Norway, and on the second Aberdeen voyage between July and September when they fish the northern banks of the North Sea, the herring catches had been good. But after their return to their home port for the East Anglian voyage the whole fleet had suffered a reverse; and by the middle of November, when there was normally at least another month of good fishing, many of the Scottish drifters that had come south with the fleet had already sailed for home in disgust.

This seasonal movement, which makes up the pattern of a drifterman's year, is one of the reasons why drifter owners have difficulty in finding crews nowadays. From the beginning of April to the middle of September a Lowestoft drifter is based in Aberdeen, with only a fortnight's trip back to Suffolk between the two Aberdeen voyages. And for the smaller drifters the months between the end of the East Anglian voyage at Christmas and the first Aberdeen voyage of the following spring are also spent away from home, either fishing for herring in the Irish Sea or for mackerel off Cornwall. Three months of the year at home is a poor inducement for a modern young man to become a drifterman, and an even poorer one for a modern girl to marry him. In the bigger drifters, like the *Suffolk Warrior*, the prospect is a little better, for between the end of one herring season at Christmas and the beginning of the next in April they go trawling in the North Sea for bottom fish, or white fish, which means that they have two nights in harbour at Lowestoft every fortnight.

The difficulty of recruiting fishermen, in spite of a special nautical course for apprentices at the local technical college, signifies the importance of other industries in Lowestoft—industries where workers are at least guaranteed their nights at home. Fishing is comparatively well paid, with the proceeds from the catch being divided between the crew and the owners, the owners taking fifty-seven per cent and the balance being again split among the crew according to a scale; in a successful year a skipper can make three thousand pounds, and a deckhand an average of twenty pounds a week. But the hours are long and the work is tough. Driftermen, though they are usually at sea only a night or two at a time, are away from home for months on end; and trawlermen, though they have forty-eight hours at home every fortnight, often have to haul their trawl in every two or three hours, day and night.

"Don't forget," said the *Suffolk Warrior*'s ship's husband, a man in a duffle coat who looked after her interests ashore, "don't forget, there's no forty-hour week for fishermen, or forty-eight hour week; it's nearer a hundred." It is not surprising that owners find it hard to get crews nowadays, and although there are young men in the trawlers, and in fact many trawler skippers are still in their twenties, the drifters are mostly manned by older men. The average age aboard the *Suffolk Warrior* was forty.

"The herring drifters are the tail end of the fishing business now," said the manager of a firm that owned both drifters and trawlers. Recently his firm had bought the last six drifters at Yarmouth, bringing the Lowestoft drifter fleet up to twenty-one. Fifty years ago, in the heyday of the herring business, there had been more than six hundred drifters at Yarmouth and Lowestoft, and during the autumn season they had been joined by over a thousand from Scotland. In those days, in each town, they say you could walk across the harbour over a solid mass of herring boats. This season Yarmouth, once the principal herring town of England, hadn't got a single drifter of its own, and had only fifty from Scotland; and Lowestoft, with five times as many trawlers as drifters, was already considering itself a white fish rather than a herring port. The huge drifter fleet of the 1913 season, nearly seventeen hundred strong, had dwindled in fifty years by just ninety-five per cent.

But something else had disappeared altogether — the invasion of Scotch fisher-girls who used to follow the herring fleet from port to port, like sheep-shearers in Australia, cleaning and curing and packing the herrings, and possibly keeping the fishermen, as they say, amused. Every guide-book mentions them — "the Scottish herring lassies who travel south in their hundreds, with their bonnets and shawls and clogs"—and it was with a faint hope of finding a few survivors that I went to Lowestoft. 'Colourful' is the favourite word for them, and no doubt much of the colour of Jumbo Fiske's own language was acquired in their company. But in 1963 there wasn't a single fisher-girl. The only Scotch women were a handful of wives of driftermen who had come south with the fleet to keep their husbands out of trouble. And the colour, apart from Jumbo's kind, was provided by the more individual of Lowestoft's own fisher-boys—by a yellow tartan mohair suit, by an electric-blue jacket, or by a pair of gold drop ear-rings.

With the fisher-girls have disappeared the acres of barrels of salted herrings that used to stretch across the denes between the cliffs and the sea, waiting for shipment to Russia and Germany, and in their place is a gigantic frozen foods factory. Only one or two herring smoke-houses remain in Lowestoft, and in the one I visited there wasn't a herring in sight, but only a lingering smell of kippers. The man there used to travel with the fleet to Storno-way and North Shields and Milford Haven and Lerwick; but now he's lucky if he can keep his Lowestoft smoke-house occupied.

"It's a good job this town doesn't still depend on the herring catch," said an old man in a pub with one eye and perhaps two teeth. "In a bad season like this it meant a bad winter for all of us." But now there are several new factories, and only a tenth of the population is engaged in the fishing business.

Fishing, however, is still very important to Lowestoft, and Waveney Street, behind the fish market, is full of offices with North Sea charts on the walls, with tremendous photographs of trawlers ploughing through gales or drifters in a silver sea, with files of Admiralty Notices to Mariners laid out for the benefit of skippers who probably never look at them, and with special entrances marked 'Crew'. Sometimes the local Member of Parliament is to be seen down at the market at eight o'clock in the morning, and although most of the business is now concerned with trawling, which is as busy as it has ever been and slowly increasing, in the autumn herring season the local newspaper still reports the daily catches of each drifter, the price obtained in the market, and the number of crans sold to freshers, freezers, red-ders and kipperers; and the Prunier Trophy, awarded every year by Madame Prunier to the drifter with the highest single night's catch during the East Anglian voyage, is still a cherished prize.

*   *   *

For three days Jumbo and the *Suffolk Warrior* stayed in harbour. Even if it hadn't been for his capstan — his four-letter little female thing of a bastard capstan — the south-west gales would have prevented him from fishing. Other drifters went out to the herring grounds in the morning, but came back again in the evening without having shot their nets, because it was too rough. For forty-eight hours there wasn't a single fresh herring to be had in Lowestoft, though this was the peak of the season.

One drifter skipper came in with a sad tale. In the gale the night before, down on the Hinder Bank off the mouth of the Scheldt, he had lost sixty nets, more than half his total, which would cost over a thousand pounds to replace. The owners cabled to their agents in Holland, in the hope that if a Dutch fishing-vessel picked up the nets they would be returned: but everyone knew that if they fell into the hands of French fishermen there wasn't a hope of getting them back.

Drifters have about a hundred nets, each fifty yards long and costing more than twenty pounds. Most of them are still made of cotton, which needs constant tanning in cutch to preserve it; they are regularly inspected, and mended in long sheds by women, or even sent to the women's homes to be repaired. Nylon nets, which don't need drying and tanning, are being introduced, but they still have to be taken out for inspection and they are unpopular both with the fishermen, who find them difficult to handle, and with the fish merchants, who complain that they cut off the herrings' heads. The Scottish driftermen have been quite successful with nylon nets, but the Lowestoft men are more conservative.

But quite apart from Jumbo's capstan and the south-west gales there was something else, a gigantic spectral problem that worried him and every other skipper and drifter owner and herring merchant in the town: the danger from the foreign herring trawlers that had been fishing for several years in the North Sea. In the good old days the British drifters had had a virtual monopoly of the herrings off north-west Europe, and a large proportion of the catch had been exported to other countries. But now those very countries—France, Belgium, Holland, Germany, Denmark, Poland, Russia—had sailed in with their own fishing fleets, and with methods that the English and Scottish fishermen considered imprudent, uneconomic, and, perhaps, unsporting. Not only did the foreigners fish the shoals of herring that migrated annually to the banks to spawn, but they had recently started 'industrial' fishing for the tiny whitebait that lived in the waters off Denmark, and which were only good for fish-meal.

"Killing the golden goose, and all that," said a drifter owner in a Lowestoft office.

"Upsetting the natural recruitment pattern of the herring age-groups," said a scientist at the fishery research laboratory along the cliff.

"Dragging their trawls over the spawning grounds, churning up the eggs, tearing my nets," said Jumbo, scattering his little four-letter words through the sentence and adding, "It's like a bloody town out there on the Hinder. On Sunday night, when the capstan broke, I counted eighty foreign trawlers." It made it no better that the Poles bought nets in England, and that some of the Russian trawlers were built in Lowestoft.

Jumbo, so they said, didn't care twopence for the scientists, though they also said that he listened to them nevertheless, if he thought there was a chance of getting a few more herrings out of it. I heard a scientist complain that people from all over the world consulted the research laboratories at Lowestoft, but seldom the local skippers. There was a deep antagonism between the scientists and the fishermen; when the scientists prophesied a figure for the herring catch and the fishermen failed to achieve it, the fishermen said that all the scientists knew about herrings was the pretty charts on their office walls, and the scientists said that the fishermen had gone to the wrong place.

Jumbo's capstan was fixed on the third evening, and he said he would sail in the morning for the Hinder Bank, and take me with him. The gale was still blowing and it would be pretty rough, he said, but I laughed; I had never been seasick in my life, and told him so; I had once been in a minesweeper about the same size as the *Suffolk Warrior*, and I could take anything after that. But Jumbo was not impressed. He too had been in the navy, in the same kind of ship, and his contempt for it was summed up in a cart-load of four-letter words. I saw that I had said the wrong thing, and after I left him I asked the ship's husband to make sure that Jumbo wouldn't be disconcerted by having a passenger on board, or feel obliged to come in after one night for my sake if he thought he could catch more herrings by staying out.

"Do you really think he would?" said the old ex-skipper. Then perhaps, I suggested, it would be a good idea to arrange to meet Jumbo in a pub that night, to make friends over a drink; but the ship's husband didn't think much of that either: "Too expensive, with Jumbo. He drinks shorts. You should just see a little glass of Drambuie in those bitts of his."

*   *   *

That night I walked down from the Lowestoft lighthouse, through a murky district of dark alleys and steep passages. I peered through the windows of a pub at the edge of the denes, which Jumbo had recommended as a place for 'goings-on', but I couldn't see anything inside and decided, in a cowardly way, to try another one. As I walked away down the dark street a man overtook me.

"What was you looking in my windows for?"

I walked on, frightened, pretending at first that I thought he was talking to somebody else, and then saying foolishly that I hadn't looked through anybody's windows.

"What was you looking in my windows for?"

I walked on through the dark, saying even more foolishly that I thought it was a pub.

"What was you looking in my windows for?"

I walked on, a little faster, while he walked beside me.

"Who is he, anyway?" shouted a woman through the night.

I walked still faster, into another street where the lights were brighter, and the man dropped back.

"Looking in my windows," shouted the man down the street.

"Who is he?" shouted the woman.

That night, presumably, Jumbo was filling up with Drambuie. That night one of his deckhands, a cunning man with dogs, was out on somebody's land, poaching a pheasant. That night, a hundred miles away on the Hinder Bank, the herrings were spawning and the foreign fishermen were hove to, preserving their trawls from the gale and waiting for daylight. And that night, five thousand miles away in Texas, where it was still early afternoon, President Kennedy was assassinated.

"What a shame," said the barmaid in the pub where I ended up, looking for a dish-cloth to mop up the mess. And the most the banners on the news-stand could say next morning was 'Lowestoft housewife gaoled'.

"What's to be, will be," said Jumbo, in the wheelhouse of the *Suffolk Warrior* as we sailed out of Lowestoft harbour in the crisp November sunshine and turned down the coast towards Belgium; there was spray beating on the esplanade and a pram being pushed in front of the grey Victorian terraces. Jumbo was genuinely, magnificently upset. Kennedy had been a good man. Jumbo honoured him with all the grief he had, which was the most he could do for anything that wasn't a herring. Throughout the day he talked about the assassination, and on the radio telephone which he constantly used to gossip across the sea with the other drifter skippers he kept bringing the subject up, laconically and mixed with fish talk: "Bad do, that, in Dallas. Good man. Got the capstan bitch mended. Lunatic, I'd say. Jim's been out two nights, hasn't got enough for breakfast. The old saying — what's to be, will be. Catch 'em on the incoming, I reckon. Poor Kennedy bloke. Bad do, that."

Algy the cook, gaunt with a face like Michael Foot, came up into the wheelhouse with mugs of tea; he had been sailing with Jumbo since the end of the war. Something about the tea made me notice how rough the sea was. There were long low ships, perhaps flat-irons bringing coal from Blyth, on the horizon, and a couple of drifters ahead on their way to the Hinder, tossing and plunging. The gale had dropped but the wind was still force five and I realised that I was feeling uncomfortable. I went and stood in the fresh air outside the wheelhouse and felt a little better, but it was cold. Waves broke over the *Suffolk Warrior*'s bows, and Kenny the hawseman came and talked to me. He had been in the navy too, and had been sent to America in the middle of the war, to bring back a new ship. The ship had been launched in Seattle, and Kenny had sailed it across to Virginia; I was getting too ill to ask just how. Kenny's geography was weak, like my stomach. They hadn't been through the Great Lakes, or the Panama Canal. Kenny wasn't sure of the route. Dallas came into it somewhere,

as it came into most things that day. Kenny left me, and I tried
to be sick but failed.

Jumbo opened the wheelhouse door and shouted to me to go
and get my dinner. I still couldn't be sick, and despondently went
down the ladder to the little mess next to the engine-room. The
crew were sitting round the table, in the middle of which lay a
plate piled with roast beef, fatty and overcooked. They made a
place for me in the corner; as I sat down I saw that I was furthest
from the door, furthest from fresh air, furthest from the sea. Algy
was busy at the stove, and brought another plate to the table—big
suet dumplings. They wobbled on the plate as the *Suffolk Warrior*
rolled. My stomach wobbled with them.

Algy put a plate of cabbage and baked potatoes in front of me,
then poured gravy all over it from an enamel jug and topped it up
with a spoonful of baked beans. He asked me if it was enough. I
looked round and saw that nobody else had baked beans, and
wondered whether Algy was trying something on. Somebody
with 'Mum' tattooed on his arm spiked a chunk of beef for me and
put it on top of my cabbage. It was like being drunk. Wildly I
spiked a dumpling, to show that there was nothing wrong with
me. I saw that my own arm had no tattoo. I tried to remember who
I had seen recently with 'Janie' tattooed in a heart; perhaps it was
Jumbo up in the wheelhouse. The gravy rocked in my plate, and
my dumpling wobbled. There was a pin-up girl on the wall, and a
wireless, and 'Mum', and margarine being spread on a loaf of
white bread by someone on the other side of the table, and the
lurching of my body against the back of the seat; and there was a
feeling, whenever I looked up across the table to the others, of
imminent catastrophe, and another feeling, whenever I looked
down at my plate, that was if anything worse.

"How d'you feel?" asked the whaleman. Somebody had told
me why he was called that, but I couldn't remember. I said I was
fine. Nobody said anything for a while.

"Well then," said the whaleman very slowly, "I was going to
say—that in that case—your looks belie your feelings."

"They say that Nelson was seasick," said the chief engineer.

"But he got his women all right," said one of the others.

"He was a crabby old bugger," said Kenny.

The chief engineer, watching me poking at my dumpling,
offered me his bunk for the afternoon, while he was on watch.

Algy took my plate away and I went down below to the crew's quarters and sat on the chief's bunk trying to decide if I had enough strength to go back up on deck again to be sick. After quarter of an hour I lay down and went to sleep. When I woke up it was dark and I was well again. I hadn't been sick. Algy brought me some tea, and I proudly ate two grilled bloaters. Nothing could make me sick now.

We were on the Hinder, and it was, as Jumbo had said, like a bloody town. There were lights all round us, trawlers everywhere. The loom of a lightship flashed on the horizon, and in the *Suffolk Warrior*'s wheelhouse Jumbo belched and switched on the echo-sounder.

The needle swept over the chart, recording a steady depth of twenty fathoms. What Jumbo was after was another mark on the chart, between the surface and the bottom, indicating herring.

The hunting began. It was a curiously primitive experience, chasing wild animals through the dark, through another element. Unlike in farming, the harvest was nothing to do with any previous operation; the fish had not been sown in the sea, the water had not been fertilised, there wasn't even any bait. It was a blind chase, with only the echo-sounder and Jumbo's intuition to guide us.

"Catch 'em on the incoming," said Jumbo. That meant he would shoot the nets at about eight o'clock. All the time he cursed the trawlers; though they had stopped fishing for the night, they were still sitting on the Hinder and getting in the way of the drifters. Looking across at the lights it was hard to think of the Russian and Polish and French crews in their ships; it was harder still to think of Dallas. But Jumbo kept on talking about it, to me and to the other skippers over the radio telephone: "Got any echoes there, Harry? Trawler bastard here, says he's not under command. Dodgy business, that Kennedy bloke. Bad do. I've got a mark on the sounder now, but it's not black. Just grey. Catch 'em on the incoming." And Jumbo began to sing softly into the microphone.

For three hours we hunted up and down, steering between the lights of the trawlers and watching the echo-sounder. The mark of herrings showed on the chart, a faint smudge that didn't satisfy Jumbo. Then suddenly, for no reason that I could see, he called up the crew to shoot the nets. With the engine stopped and the mizzen sail blowing the *Suffolk Warrior* ahead, the nets were pulled out of the hold and over the side. It was hard work, hand over hand, to keep up with the speed of the ship. Sixty-one nets were shot, a mile and a half in length, hanging in the water like a long tennis net supported by orange plastic floats. The warps were made fast, and we all turned in to sleep, except Jumbo in the wheelhouse and one man on watch.

For half the night the *Suffolk Warrior* drifted with the tide across the Hinder Bank, the mizzen sail keeping her head to wind and the net stretching through the water, suspended between the surface and the bottom. If there were shoals of herring about, they would swim into the net. If it was too rough or too cold they would stay down on the bottom and probably be caught the next day by the foreign trawlers. If the *Suffolk Warrior* drifted too close to one of the foreigners, Jumbo stood to lose more than a thousand pounds of equipment. If he went back to Lowestoft with only five crans like last time, the week's work—thanks to the capstan—would show a loss of five hundred pounds. If that smudge on the echo-sounder chart didn't get any blacker, if that seasick passenger in his new fisherman's jersey was the Jonah he looked, if the capstan broke down again and they had to haul the nets by hand, if the late night weather forecast gave another gale warning, there was nothing Jumbo could do but heave his great stomach away from the wheel and deliver another burst of little four-letter words. And all the time there was that bad do in Dallas to talk about with the other drifter skippers on the Hinder.

Then, before midnight, the radio telephone broke down, cutting the *Suffolk Warrior* off. Jumbo thumped it in vain, and the pressure of those little words in his huge body forced a small torrent of them out into the wheelhouse, spilling like herrings from a basket.

Herrings—nobody could tell if there were any there. The smudge on the chart wasn't very promising, and anyway the echo-sounder was not infallible. Another Lowestoft drifter came within hailing distance and a Suffolk voice swept across the black water, cursing; the skipper hadn't even bothered to shoot his nets, it was so unhopeful. These trawler bastards. And that Kennedy bloke being shot like that.

At one in the morning Algy shouted down to wake the crew. The tea was up; the old man was going to haul. I went up to the wheelhouse and watched through the windows as the capstan wound in the heavy bottom warp and the crew pulled the nets in over the side. A few herrings, caught by the gills in the mesh, flashed in the deck lights. Jumbo swore, and the gulls screamed. Ten nets came in, then twenty, and it looked like another bad catch. The *Suffolk Warrior* tossed on the waves, while the men kept their balance and stowed the nets and floats in the hold. The pile of herrings, shaken out and collecting in the corners of the deck, began to look more promising.

Thirty nets came in, and forty, and then imperceptibly the number of herrings coming over the side increased. Things were looking up. After the gales and the foreign trawlers and the capstan — after Dallas — Jumbo at last was going to be avenged.

And then the capstan broke. Jumbo Fiske, for the first time since I met him, was speechless; there were no words left. The chief engineer brought a five-gallon drum of oil to pour into the hydraulic mechanism, but after a few more turns it had all leaked into the bilges. Those mechanics ashore had mucked up their job. Three-quarters of the total nets were in, but the rest, which seemed to be full of fish, were still lying in the sea.

We pulled in the last fourteen nets by hand, the whaleman and I on the bottom warp doing the capstan's job and the rest shaking the herrings out of the nets. Algy the cook was stationed down in the rope locker, standing in the middle and giddily coiling the warp round himself as he hauled it in. Jumbo, alone up in the wheelhouse, began to recover his speech, and the little words came hailing down to the deck again, encouraging and kindly.

The whaleman offered me his gloves, but I refused them. It was fun, in the night, standing on the tossing foredeck and pulling on the warp, with gulls clamouring round the ship and herrings by the thousand coming in over the side. Somebody produced mugs of cocoa, and Kenny said, "Roll on bloody Christmas" — when the *Suffolk Warrior* would give up drifting and go trawling till the spring.

The herrings, a foot deep on the deck, slipped backwards and forwards as the ship rolled, a silver liquid mass touched with blue and red. While we drank our cocoa the two young deckhands got out wooden spades and shovelled the catch through a hole into the fish-hold below. The last few nets were pulled in, laden heavily with fish, as dawn was breaking over the Dutch coast. Algy's ring of rope was piled above his head, and I had fish scales

Skegness
Twisters

Skegness Middle-aged

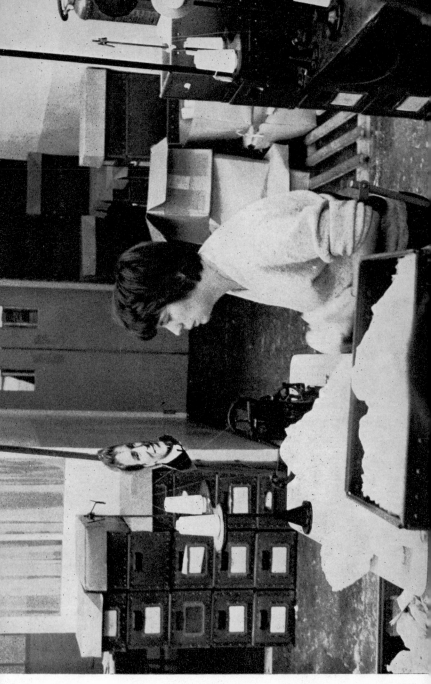

Leek
Pin-up

Liverpool Dock

*Liverpool
Cavern Club*

Liverpool Sunset

Chertsey Commuters

Corby Ore Train

Burnley Policeman

Newmarket Spectators

on my face and blisters on my fingers, but I hadn't been seasick.

Forty-two crans was the total catch, and half of them had been hauled in by hand. I went below and slept on the watchman's bunk while the crew worked for another hour, packing the herrings into aluminium boxes. There had been fears that the old man would want to shoot again, and I half hoped he would; but when the crew turned in at last they said we were already on our way back to Lowestoft.

As we sailed in through the harbour entrance, twenty-four hours after leaving, I was sitting in the mess eating fresh herrings in my fingers, like Jumbo the first time I saw him. Through the port-hole I saw the ship's husband standing on the quay, perplexed at the *Suffolk Warrior*'s return, and suddenly a voice bellowed from the wheelhouse above me: " . . . capstan . . . bastard . . ." The little four-letter words rang round the harbour and the ship's husband turned up the collar of his duffle coat.

A sample box of herrings was ready on deck, and as soon as the *Suffolk Warrior* was alongside it was handed up to a man who ran with it along the quay to the auction room at the corner of the drifter basin. Another man rang a bell, and the merchants left the market to bid for the catch. The fish were tipped on to a table, the men's breath vaporised in the cold morning air, the auctioneer rubbed his hands and coughed, and I thought I recognised one or two faces from the Ludlow cattle market. The bidding went up from thirteen pounds a cran to fourteen and then to fifteen, and at last another sixteen shillings. The *Suffolk Warrior* had earned more than six hundred pounds that night, but the other Lowestoft drifters had caught only three or four crans each; not enough for Jumbo's breakfast.

IX

LIVERPOOL

THE best view of Liverpool is, for many people, the first—from a ship in the middle of the Mersey, before docking. One Saturday morning in early December I sat drinking tea in the wheelhouse of a tug, waiting to meet a ship coming up the river, and wondered how wrong an impression one could get. The liver birds perched on the tallest office building, the smudge of the Cathedral tower looking faintly Hindu in the distance, the funnels and masts behind the dock wall, the Gothic warehouses of Bootle, the gantries of Birkenhead, the stumps of the New Brighton tower (Blackpool's rival that had to be felled because it was unsafe), the Wallasey ferry and Irish packet and Canadian liner and Liberian super-tanker forming their slow patterns across the viscous surface—it looked pretty good.

"Nice day," said the tugmaster, meaning much more than the weather. He loved that view, though like many Liverpudlians he hadn't been born on Merseyside. He wasn't even Irish or Welsh or Scots. He came from Devon, the son of a Brixham fisherman, but he belonged to Liverpool now. His own son, the chief engineer of a tanker in the Persian Gulf, spoke Scouse like a native.

Our ship came in from the sea, a towering freighter flying the flag of Switzerland.

"Eight thousand tons of flipping Gruyère cheese," said the tug's mate in the corner of the wheelhouse, looking up from the back page of the *Daily Echo*. I hadn't really been aware of him before; this was the first time he had spoken. "You live in Chelsea, squire? they're playing Everton today. Be a good game. Chelsea's good, like." That little suffix creeps in everywhere in Liverpool.

The tug nudged the freighter's stern and the deck-boy passed a hawser up to a face hanging over the rail. Not a word was spoken, in either Swiss or Scouse. With another tug at the bow and a couple of toots on a whistle the ship was handed smoothly, perfectly, through a lock into the Gladstone Dock and berthed next to the *Mauretania*. As the warps were being made fast the tug-master picked up the radio telephone and asked his office across the Mersey for orders. Nothing till midnight, came the reply.

"Everton for me," said the mate.

Ashore, beyond the dockyard gates — gates that must have been built with Holloway Prison in mind — there are the first hints that not everything in Liverpool is as fine as the view from the middle of the Mersey; but one's early suspicions are outweighed (and in the face of the sheer tonnage of it all, outweighed beyond recovery) by the warehouses — giants' palaces, mediaeval fortresses, massive temples of brickwork that, like the course at Aintree, can be measured in furlongs. "Mosley says house Britons first," was painted on a wall, and the tobacco warehouse alone could accommodate every one of them in style.

Walking towards the middle of the city, so stunned is one by the size of the buildings that one can only slowly perceive the change that has occurred in the air. Out in the river it was clear, but here in the streets it is opaque and very dirty. It is as if one has been pushed ten degrees of latitude into the northern murk; and pushed, likewise, fifty years back into the past. The murk hangs over Liverpool's black buildings, made of something like coal, and the past pervades the curious imperial quality of the city. Liverpool's bankers, ship-owners and underwriters, in their sahib days, carried their splendid architecture to the outposts of the world; but the grandeur of the prototypes at home is smothered by the gloom. A marble banking hall might almost be in Lagos, a grand arcade through a shipping building might be in Singapore, an open-air staircase of an old office block might be in Calcutta. But there are no fans twisting overhead in the bank, the arcade echoes with the bronchial Liverpool cough, and the gilt ironwork of the staircase is overlaid with grime.

"Up that street till you get to a dirty big black building," said a man I stopped to ask the way. He meant Saint George's Hall, and it is so dirty, big and black that one hardly believes it can be hollow. It stands in the middle of Liverpool's acropolis, between the pinnacles of Lime Street station and the monumental mouth of the Mersey tunnel, surrounded by lions and heroes; opposite it, stretching from the bus station to the Duke of Wellington, is the long dark stoa of the museum, library and art gallery.

The John Moores biennial exhibition of contemporary painting was still on in the gallery, but to me the restless incomprehensibilities and strident rubbish of many of the pictures seemed inept for Liverpool. On a table was a photograph of the prize-winning artist aiming a kick at his own canvas and quoted as saying, "They are terrible pictures; no wonder mine won." It was a relief to get out into the rooms of the permanent collection, to Andromeda chained to the rocks, to the death of Lord Nelson, to Dante's first sight of Beatrice. At least these fitted more happily into Liverpool; it is a kind of pre-Raphaelite city, left out in the rain and the dirt when it should have been put behind glass.

This feeling of solid out-of-dateness is reflected in some of the pubs round Dale Street; in the men in bowler hats tucking into shrimps and mussels and plates of red roast beef; in the photos of tall-funnelled steamers on their first voyage through the Panama Canal; in the stout waitress leaning over a balcony and shouting, "Any oysters left, John?"; in the notice, "Gentlemen are requested not to smoke before 2.30 p.m."; and in the clusters of plasterwork on the ceilings and marble-topped bars and engraved mirrors, not deliberately preserved as they would be in London, but simply still going strong.

Yet even here, in the heart of Liverpool, there is a touch of uneasiness in the air. Perhaps it's the queer feeling one gets that, because nothing seems to have happened in Liverpool for fifty years (except the bombing) there is some ghastly cataclysm brewing up; or perhaps it's just the quantities of policemen standing around in pairs, with Alsatians at their heel.

"It's like Johannesburg, really," said a shipping man in the plush comfort of the Palatine Club. "Same guilt feeling. And with the same good reason."

Liverpool's conscience besets the city as thickly as the slums. You have only to walk a short way from Dale Street and you are in the world of bedroom slippers on the cobbles, of Z-cars and Oxo cubes and Typhoo tea, and of huge posters standing among the dereliction and proclaiming 'Build with the Conservatives'. The irony is not in the posters, but in the fact that six of Liverpool's nine Members of Parliament are Conservatives, and the reasons for voting for them, like the rusting tramlines that remain in many of the city's streets, lie deep. One man told me he thought it was the result of a tradition of paternalism, which reserved the responsibilities of government for the great families — rich, liberal, confident — and left to the ordinary Liverpudlians the more exciting business that had to be settled between one street and the next, between Catholics and Orangemen, or Welsh and Scots, or supporters of Everton and Liverpool City. And the old barrier dividing the patricians from the plebs is not only responsible for the extraordinary amount of social work done by the former, but also for the extraordinary unsophistication of the latter; charity, like the grime, smothers Liverpool in proportion to distress.

But whereas in the grand old days the rich lived in their big houses round Sefton Park and the rest of society fell into place in an accepted hierarchy, nowadays anybody who can afford it has bought a house in the fresh air of the Wirral peninsula to which he drives through the Mersey tunnel at five-thirty every evening, and the traditional pattern is breaking. Three-quarters of a million people, with their fair share of passions and more than their share of poverty, remain in a community that is both proud and abject alike. Violence may be the keynote, whether in the contrast between Dale Street and the slums or in the turmoil that rumbles everywhere and explodes in street-corner brawls and bottle-battles at football matches, and that can be heard pulsing through the rhythm of the Mersey Sound; but violence means vitality, and though a visitor may sometimes feel frightened he can never be indifferent. Liverpool is a city of expatriates dumped in a corner of Lancashire where they don't belong, who have joined in a wild haphazard way and made something original out of it. It is not only the view from the middle of the Mersey that reminds one of descriptions of Shanghai in the thirties. As an English town it has a quality — whether it's black sheep or golden boy — of being different.

Some visitors, disgusted by the provincial snobbery and bleak facilities of the city, can't wait to get out. I met a girl who was appalled equally at the ritual dinner parties she found herself attending and at the lack of restaurants. There are scores of Chinese eating-places, but as almost everybody orders fish and chips anyway, the food is as tawdry and inevitable as the crimson lanterns and willow-pattern wallpaper. The Liverpudlians, she complained, were for ever boasting of their art gallery and philharmonic hall and their three theatres; but there wasn't a delicatessen shop or a decent coffee house on the whole of Merseyside.

Besides, of the three theatres that week, one was offering Olde Tyme Music Hall, another had *Hay Fever*, and the third was closed pending *Robinson Crusoe*.

But other newcomers love it, even if there is a suspicion of self-defence in their enthusiasm.

"I wouldn't live anywhere else now," said the secretary of the Chamber of Commerce, a Londoner. "There's just this dreadful whispering campaign against Liverpool; it's doing us a lot of harm, stopping people building factories and opening offices here." Another thing that saddened him was the decline of the small family businesses — tramp owners, fruit brokers, oil seed merchants — that had been passed from father to son since Liverpool's golden days and that had handed on from one generation to the next more than just a comfortable job and a loyal staff. They had each tended to specialise in their chosen region of the world, concentrating on a corner of Asia or a stretch of African coast or a handful of South American republics; but now the trade was falling more and more into the hands of the big companies who could never get to know the territory as thoroughly or as lovingly as the small firms. "Pity, I think," said the secretary.

"I've got the best job in the world," said a man who had once looked after sledge dogs in the Antarctic but had exchanged them for a desk on the top floor of a shipping office where he could watch the kestrels nesting in one of the towers of the Royal Liver building.

"Better schools up here than down at Dagenham," said a man at the huge new Ford factory, who had already been adopted as prospective Conservative candidate in one of the city's constituencies.

"The people are so friendly," said a Scotsman, like a white man among the natives. "They're genuine, you know. Say what they mean, and all that sort of thing. None of the deviousness of your southerners."

The city planning officer, after fifteen years with the London County Council and one year in Liverpool, found it very refreshing, though there were drawbacks: "I do miss my friends. I was very comfortable in Blackheath." To him the fact that Liverpool was still where London had been in 1945 was not its problem but its opportunity, and the years of dereliction and delay only meant that it could profit by the experience of other town plans. He felt

that Liverpool was the optimum size for a town, and with everybody—the city council, the business men, the public who wrote
endlessly to the local papers—he had found nothing but excitement at the idea of a plan. Already the first building was going up
which incorporated an arrangement for a second shopping level
to be built later, and soon a chaotic area round the market
opposite Lime Street station was to be demolished and developed.
He was sure that once the work was begun it would generate its
own enthusiasm; and even though the whole town plan might
not be finished by the end of the century—in so far as any town
plan is ever finished—and even though it was meaningless without a central plan for the whole of Merseyside that could disregard
the petty bickerings of neighbouring town councils and adopt a
policy for the development of the area, he saw it as much more
than just a solution to the traffic problem and a substitution of
new buildings for old.

Listening to him I was infected by the vision of a feckless
society, landed with a legacy of devastation and apathy, discover-
ing in a modern town plan something of the purposefulness that
had been shattered by the bombs and something of the responsibility that, with a receding economy, a dwindling faith and a
retreating oligarchy, could restore a little of Liverpool's self-
respect.

Liverpool is sensitive to its reputation, and it is significant that
the name Coventry is so much on people's lips. Coventry made
its town plan fifteen years ago, has already got its shopping centre
and seen its cathedral bombed and rebuilt; while Liverpudlians
have only one brash post-war shopping street and look impatiently up the hill to their Gothic monster, like an out-dated
battleship on the stocks, laid down sixty years ago and still
unfinished.

"We've just got to live with it," said the city planning officer,
meaning the new shopping street, though he might equally have
meant the cathedral.

"But what can you expect?" said a social worker, explaining
Liverpool's six per cent unemployment figure. "Coventry is a
manufacturing town. In Liverpool only a third of the working
population is engaged in manufacturing. This town is built on a
tripod—commerce, transport and distribution—and when things
go wrong in other parts of the country we feel it here too." When

a Lancashire cotton mill closes down or a company sells a couple of transatlantic liners or a merchant moves his South American business to London, it affects Liverpool. And because many of its own industries — soap, rubber, chemicals — are those which require only a small proportion of skilled workers, Liverpool has the lowest recruitment of apprentices for skilled trades in the whole of north-west England. Most manufacturing towns can employ, and therefore train, a reasonable amount of artisans; it is a measure of Liverpool's vulnerability that even white-collar workers live precariously, and recently, with the appearance of bingo and betting offices all over the country, many hundreds who worked for the big football pools at Liverpool have been thrown out of work. New factories are appearing slowly, but although the biggest, the Ford factory, will eventually employ over ten thousand workers, only about three hundred of them will be skilled tradesmen and the prospect for ambitious young men is bleak. So is the hope of a quick reduction in unemployment; when sixty men recently left their factory to go and work at Ford's they were not replaced at the old firm because, by modernising its plant, it could do without them.

The Ford factory, so they say, is the most modern in the country, by which they mean it is the newest. Its designers studied car factories all over the world, and the result is a nightmare. Thirty-eight million pounds, three hundred and forty-six acres of pressing and welding and painting and assembling and trimming and testing, enough bricks to stretch from London to Aberdeen, enough hot water to keep one million and fifty-two thousand kettles permanently on the boil, a potential production of eleven hundred cars a day — the statistics roll as smoothly round the public relations office as the cars roll down the assembly line.

That assembly line — it terrified me; and it terrified a lot of Liverpudlians too. Working on it was quite unlike anything else in the experience of most Merseyside workers, who were baffled at the speed and continuous activity of a car factory. Chasing a car body moving steadily past one, trying to screw a pair of head-lamps on to it and fix the radiator and windscreen before it has moved out of one's pitch and another car body has moved in, was a very different matter from throwing a hawser round a bollard or working in a warehouse; and a lot of workers left Ford's after a few frantic, hellish days. But gradually the word went round

Liverpool that jobs there were hard but well paid, tiring but clean, and thousands more men have applied to work there than can ever be employed. And so unusual is the work that the factory is besieged by people who want to go round it, and the company runs free tours every day for the public—for men who wish they could get a job there, and for women who want to see just exactly what their husbands do all day.

*   *   *

Modernisation is a word that can scarcely have been heard in the Scouse vocabulary until quite recently, and the novelty of it, with its suggestion of excitement and revolt, may be one reason for the sensational local treatment of those masters of monotony, archpriests of din, the Beatles. In Liverpool it is difficult not to be bludgeoned into thinking that the Beatles are really something important in the Merseyside scene, in the line of Liverpool's famous sons alongside Gladstone, Tommy Handley and the Braddocks, and not just the latest in a series of ephemeral rock 'n' roll groups, this year's model to be traded in for something new next year. Before long, as they admit themselves, they will be as dead as the liver birds; but if they prove to have any more staying power than other pop singers it can only be due, not to any musical superiority, but to clever exploitation by people twice their age, to their own disarming vitality, and to the optimism of their songs after such a long spell of unrequital. "She loves you," they yell to their fans, when all these years we have been told she doesn't; and the obvious reaction is to scream with happiness.

In Liverpool, as elsewhere, the Beatles smother the bookstalls, they monopolise the front page of the evening paper, they decorate the pubs, they are woven into nylon stockings, and when, between royal commands and foreign tours, they fit in a rare appearance in their home town, the city police force lines up round the Odean cinema, and if you don't belong to the fan club and can't scream you might as well stay at home and watch them on the box. But to Liverpudlians they are also 'our' Beatles, everybody's darlings, treated as a personal fulfilment.

"One of the Beatles lives down that street," said a taxi-driver proudly, and then slightly anxiously he added, "You've heard of the Beatles, haven't you?" as though worried that perhaps I

*4

hadn't. And a very distinguished city father, unable to tell the difference between an embarrassment and a godsend—or between a Beatle and a Braddock—referred possessively though obliquely to "the effect of what we might call, er, the Beatles". Regretfully he put the spate of pop singers down to poverty and to the necessity of self-reliance by which Liverpudlians have always had to entertain themselves; but the local boy in him liked the idea of Liverpool, already the home of the world's most famous steeple-chase, begetting four such illustrious sons.

"Of course, you've been to the Cavern," said a businessman, as somebody in Sydney might say, "Of course, you've seen the bridge." And of course, I had. "This is it, the home of the Beatles," was stuck over the door of a warehouse in a narrow street in the middle of the city. The bouncer, an immense man filling the doorway, interrogated me briefly and then shifted to let me in. At the bottom of a stone staircase, a young man at a desk was taking money, three-and-six from members and four-and-six from me. He said it was the biggest club in England, with sixteen thousand members paying a shilling a year to belong. Officially there was a minimum age limit of seventeen, but he admitted they were not strict about it. "If any of the kids look very young—you know, very young indeed—we let them in, but we tell them to bring along their birth certificates next time." He thought that the reason why they had so little trouble at the Cavern was that the members were so young. Except on Saturday nights, when older gangs sometimes tried to break in, or when the police had to be called to stop the crowds blocking the traffic in the street outside, there was nothing that the bouncer couldn't deal with on his own.

Half the sixteen thousand members seemed to be there that night, and most of them seemed under age. By the light of an electric bulb about thirty yards away I could make out three long brickwork vaults, tunnels choked with smoke and noise, and in the distance a group, three guitarists and a drummer, standing on a platform hurling decibels into their microphones. The yells and throbs and twangs roared down the vaults; and when the group stopped to announce another number the kids screamed till I thought the brick roof would crack.

Somewhere there was a Coca-Cola bar and a cloakroom, and there was a lot of dancing, and in the dark corners of the cellar a little kissing. "We don't get much snogging, like," said the man at the desk "and anyway, there's not much room for anything expressive." And anyway, most of them looked too young.

The dancing was the important thing, after the screaming. It wasn't very complicated or very energetic — just a gentle twitching of arms and bottoms — but many of the girls, and some of the boys for that matter, were marvellous to look at. Youth, when it is healthy and well-dressed and enjoying itself to the verge of ecstasy, can hardly fail to be beautiful. But very few seemed to have crossed the verge, and on most faces there was a look of sublime vacuity. Perhaps I should have been at the Cavern in the days of the Beatles.

"They haven't been here for months," said the manager. But the next night the Rattles from Hamburg were coming, Germany's answer to the Beatles, and he was expecting a big crowd.

Outside in the street a number of kids without the money to go in were squatting on the pavement listening to the noise coming up the ventilator, like untouchables at a temple, frantic for every scrap of bliss granted by the gods inside. This was hallowed ground, where the Beatles began.

The Cavern is only one of dozens of clubs in Liverpool, booming with the Mersey Sound and brightening the nights. At the Downbeat the bouncer at the door wouldn't let me in, and at the Blue Angel, where people dress in leather and drink vodka and orange, I watched a girl lose ten of her boy's sixpences in the fruit machine and then ask for more. At Hope Hall, near the university, favoured by the students and decorated with paintings rejected by the John Moores exhibition, 'happenings', despite the reputation, hardly ever happen, and there was the same noise and same smell as at the Cavern — the same faces too, but with a little more green eye-shadow on the girls and a few more whiskers on the boys. At the Mardi Gras, where there was a small crowd of non-members standing outside the door and twitching silently to the rhythm coming from inside, I had more trouble with the bouncer; and at the Gaslight, after watching a girl with magenta hair go in, I didn't even dare to ring the bell.

*   *   *

But the Mersey Sound, despite its violent beat, is only a whisper to the authentic voice of Liverpool, though Scouse, like so much else in the city, also takes a bit of getting used to. When Ford's tried to find two hundred men at Dagenham to take key jobs in their new factory at Liverpool they got few volunteers, and they had to make a special film about Merseyside and run lectures on its merits and bus tours for the men and their families to inspect it before they got the number; but once the two hundred men were established, not one of them returned to Essex. They fell, as so many others have done, to the curious attraction of being Liverpudlians.

Liverpool, even more than other big ports, has a feeling of belonging to the world, though it is no longer the world centre of the raw cotton trade, and though Britannia on the dome of the elegant city hall sits a little self-consciously these days. With such a big population of immigrants and sailors it is not surprising that so many people in the town have such improbable information — the cost of living in Buenos Aires, the labour conditions in Auckland, the latest pop disc in San Francisco, the price of watches in Honolulu, the price of women in Bangkok.

"If there's a dock strike today in Adelaide," said a police sergeant I met walking through the docks, "it's ten to one they knew about it last night in Bootle."

For a visitor Liverpool was both depressing and exciting. And, perhaps above all, it was memorable. I stayed only eight nights there, but I slept in four hotels, from the cavernous marble pretensions of the Adelphi, with massive sanitary-ware and a feeling of extravagant obsolescence peculiar to railway property, to a place in Mount Pleasant where I had a tiny room in the middle of the building, with no outside wall and no window; the air, or rather the smell of frying onions, came in under the door, and the only way of telling whether the night had turned to day was when the onions turned to bacon.

Liverpool was memorable for its vitality as for its archaism, for its stultifying grime as for its variety. I remember the advertisements for fan clubs and a Cadillac in the *Mersey Beat*, the weekly paper devoted entirely to the Mersey Sound; and I remember my surprise at finding "When did you last see your father?" in the city art gallery, when all this time I had thought it was a waxwork at Madame Tussaud's. Somewhere there were two nuns standing, incomprehensibly, in the doorway of a cocktail lounge; and in a pub, or a club or a Chinese restaurant or a Wimpy bar, there was a girl with mauve hair and a boy with 'England for ever' tattooed on the back of his hand. She said to him, "I'm going to London after Christmas. For three months. To do a course. Massaging." And he protested feebly, but she interrupted: "Now I've told you before. You'd better start finding yourself another girl friend. You've got till Christmas. Besides, you're old to me. Twenty-five. That's ancient."

There were the Irish everywhere, but particularly in the pubs, and somehow doubly Irish for being in Liverpool; there's nobody better than an Irishman in Liverpool, and he shouts it in a voice rich with beer and passion. And there were the strangers everywhere—Russians? Poles? or just the Irish again? Twice a day I was stopped in the street and asked the way. And there was also the foreign language everywhere—Turkish? Afrikaans? I kept turning round to listen, but it was only Scouse again; I simply hadn't recognised it, and hadn't believed that English could sound so ugly.

There were the London landmarks—Hatton Garden, Pall Mall, Fleet Street, Covent Garden, Whitechapel, Islington, Wapping. There was the awful feeling that one had seen the red brick Prudential building in Dale Street before, as if the one in Holborn had been sent up to Liverpool, like a director from the head office being sent to the provinces to clear up a bit of local trouble. There was the Main Bridewell in Cheapside, no less grim than the office blocks and much less grimy; there was the black Greek façade of the public library, and behind it an organisation that for facilities and design would put my own local library in London to shame; and there was the market, so oriental that one felt constrained to haggle.

In the distance, through the murk, ever-palpable as the Mersey, was the tower of the Anglican cathedral, built by a meat millionaire and reminiscent not so much of a Gothic tower as that of an immense Shiva temple; and up the hill by the university was the Catholic cathedral, being erected like a concrete missile on its launching pad, something sent over from Cape Kennedy to defend the Western alliance.

One cannot generalise about Liverpool except to say that, just as Liverpudlians are neither Lancashire nor Irish nor Welsh nor Chinese nor West Indian nor Protestant nor Catholic, so also their city is unique. And for a visitor that winter there was a feeling of

momentousness far more exciting than the raucous fashions of the
Cavern Club. The huge devastated areas between Paradise Street
and the river, unchanged since the bombs dropped, and the difficulties of a town spreading into the territory of half a dozen
councils and two counties, were matched by a bold and brilliant
plan for the city centre and the likelihood of a central policy for
the development of the whole of Merseyside.

"They've seen a thing or two in their time," said the tugmaster
out in the middle of the Mersey, nodding across at the liver birds
on their pinnacles. "But nothing to what's coming."

"It can't change Everton, skipper," said the mate. "They'll go
on winning, like, whatever happens."

X

SUTTON HOLLOW

CHRISTMAS came, bringing its ritual of food and presents. I went to midnight mass in an old village abbey by the Thames — fur hats in the pews, coughing among the carols, candles un-flickering in a cold brass chandelier — and for a few days it froze very hard. When it had started to thaw I went for a walk and saw a boy bicycling miraculously across a lake; the ice had begun to melt, the surface was already water, and the wheels of his bicycle cast a little rippling wake between himself and his reflection.

Though it had begun, for me, in a holiday camp in August and was to end in a Lancashire casino a week before Easter, it was turning out to be a perfectly ordinary winter in England. As I travelled round the country, it was the uneventfulness that was most impressive. England seemed a country bereft of drama, where the age of affluence had banished hardship, and passion had been swallowed in a gigantic yawn; if nobody seemed to be loving each other very much, nobody was hating each other either. Even the prospect of a general election only a few months ahead, with the possibility of an end to thirteen years' Conservative rule, seemed to arouse neither hope nor dread. For me, by nature embarrassed by the whiff of quarrelsomeness and inclined to run away at the sound of a raised voice, this national apathy was not as galling as it might have been to other people; and in fact some of its symptoms (no photos of the boss everywhere as there would be in so many other countries, and in fact no public heroes, except the Beatles) I found rather nice. Other things were rather nasty, and certainly the nastiest was the food.

Travellers in England — most of whom are commercial travel-lers and stay in the same sort of places that I stayed in — are sub-jected to even worse cooking than I had expected. Perhaps because I eat so well at home, perhaps because in London one is deceived by the delicatessen shops and Italian coffee bars and Indian restaurants and evidence of foreign travel, I had thought that the English palate was becoming more sensitive than it had been. But the meals I ate—from the great grey greasy breakfasts with jelly marmalade on sliced bread and strong tea or weak coffee as often as not poured from a pot that advertises cigarettes, to the tinned suppers of oxtail soup, fruit salad and synthetic ice-cream— quickly undeceived me. In restaurants it was no better, where potato chips and tinned peas are laid beside everything from mixed grills to egg foo-yong as inevitably as a knife and fork. And not even the rubber plants and dangling chianti bottles in the more pretentious places, nor the soiled tablecloths and smell of fat in the humbler ones, nor the surly ungracious service in them all, were more distressing than the difficulty of getting a simple glass of water. The travellers of England should be honoured for the way they take the plates of cold roast meat heated up with gravy ("Pork or beef, dear?" and you get the one you didn't ask for), the wet puddings and custard, the humming waitresses with their sniffs and dirty sleeves and ridiculous familiarity—if only they didn't take it all so uncomplainingly.

For me the best food in England that winter was in a cottage at Sutton Hollow, below the north escarpment of the Sussex downs, where a painter called Tom cooks dishes he has found in the villages of Provence and Calabria and Sardinia. His clogs clump-ing on the brick floor, his eyes rolling with the remembrance of things eaten late one Mediterranean night, his voice quivering like his nostrils at the whiff of mutton hissing in the wood smoke or of herbs stewing in a sauce, his loaves of home-baked bread and pots of home-made marmalade and pickles of home-grown damsons stored among his paintings of red-tiled churches and whitewashed streets, his talk of books and friends and music and Latin laughter and back again to food—his hospitality for a few winter days was as benignant as a trip to France or Italy.

For those days, too, Tom managed to rustle up a little sunshine, bright almost as in Provence, to warm the chestnut ploughed fields and light up a copper tree in the distant purple woods. And for good measure, after a dazzling day when the dusk brought a hard edge like a water-colour to the crest of the old chalk downs, we found a pair of roe deer bucking their white rumps and dodg-ing into a copse.

Tom is a foreigner in Sutton Hollow, like most of the other inhabitants of the district, and the natives are becoming almost as rare as the roe deer. One of the last is his nearest neighbour, Daisy, a tiny L-shaped woman with a face as bent as her body, who stands inside her open doorway busying herself with cat food and making the most of her last days in the little thatched cottage where seventy-five years ago she was born. It has been the only home in her life, she says, twisting her head sideways and upwards to talk to anybody who comes to her door; and though she was once a governess in Plymouth and during the Great War made munitions at Woolwich Arsenal, she was never very happy away from Sutton Hollow. She wouldn't go back to London again for all the world. But a year ago, alone in her cottage, she had a stroke, and while she was in hospital they came and took away her two cows and eighteen of her nineteen cats. Now she hasn't even got the strength to prune the japonica she once planted outside her cottage door, and though she did manage recently to walk a quarter of a mile to the end of the Hollow to watch a farmer milk his Jersey cows, she nearly collapsed walking back again; it is years since she last went up on top of the downs, where she picked cowslips as a girl, and very soon she won't even have the pleasure of feeding the birds in her doorway or of watching the seasons at work in her own little field. Last summer, after she came back from hospital, a man from Bognor came to the door and offered her three thousand pounds for her cottage, and Daisy sadly sold it to him.

When they heard of the money her relations, who had left her alone all these years, pounced. Some cousins in Brighton who had never bothered her before, wrote and asked her to go and live with them; and a niece in another village along the downs, the daughter of Daisy's brother who had never taken any interest in the cottage at Sutton Hollow, went to see a solicitor and successfully claimed a share of the cash.

Daisy applied to the county council for a flat in Petworth, but she so dreads the thought of living in even such a drowsy, gentle little town as that, that she still lingers in her cottage while she can. Almost every week the Bognor man's wife drives over impatiently to see if Daisy shows signs of moving out; but though she comforts herself that even from a flat in Petworth it won't be impossible to hobble out into the fields again, she finds it hard to make the effort to pack up; and reluctantly she has told her successors that they may bring in their workmen even before she has gone, to start on their improvements to her old cottage and make it a fit residence for the modern Sussex.

So even while old Daisy lives there, she may yet see the arrival of a carved rustic name-board at the end of the garden path, a brass carriage lamp by the cottage door, a thatched bird-table and a sham water well with bucket and chain in the garden to counterbalance the electric machinery indoors. Her cottage might even have the indignity, like the farmhouse down the road, of a reconditioned London street lamp, converted from gas and hung above the porch, to bring back to Daisy those hated days at the munitions factory.

Daisy is one of the few surviving Sussex people in the district, and with the farms being bought by gentlemen from outside and mechanised to reduce the pay-roll, the younger generation is moving to the factories of Horsham and Crawley and Chichester. The Sussex accent is going the way of the cart-horse, and the neo-villagers belong no more to the country than the swarthy servants they import specially from Galicia.

"They're not the nine-to-five boys round here," said Tom. "They're the big fish, the ones that get to their London offices only an hour or so before lunch. You should see the cars lined up in Pulborough station yard."

"We're going up to London tomorrow, to Cruft's," said a loud female voice through a laurel hedge; and another one out of a car window stopped me and asked if this was the way to Duncton, and when I said I didn't know, it asked if there was a steep hill along here, and when I said I thought there were plenty, the window was quickly wound up and the car driven off in disgust.

Haughty ladies ride on high horses along the roads, waving their whips at the traffic; and from the grey Gothic castle standing in the woods, now divided into flats, people exercise their poodles. Once a year the Morris dancers perform outside the village pub, but there isn't a bumpkin among them, only barristers and architects and Shell men — as Tom says, "*New Statesmen* readers, all of them."

The reproduction Georgian door-knockers were glinting in the winter sun, and beyond the first snowdrops in Sutton churchyard builders were at work on the rambling old rectory. It had been sold for a colossal price, and perhaps will once again become the focus of social life, with parties through the french windows and laughter out among the wellingtonias. Already the vicar has moved to a new red brick house next door, more appropriate to a modern stipend, more labour-saving, and of course much more Georgian.

In a neighbouring village inn one may come across an old gaffer with a tangled beard and gold rings in his ears, a relic preserved in the public bar; but there is also a photo of him over the bar, holding a pint of beer, for he is quaint, another antique to attract the customers along with the copper warming-pan, and soon old men like him will not only be preserved but specially turned out for the trade – reproduction gaffers.

"Do you remember . . . ?" the gaffer asks another man, speaking of the past, and for a moment one has a vision of an age-old Sussex life that is almost gone. "Do you remember old Winnie Allen? When she was dead, lying on her back, she was as tall as when she'd been standing up alive. Nineteen stone, she was . . ." – but the bloodies and the buggers are dropped too often to convince a hardened stranger, as implausible as the collection of policemen's truncheons on the wall.

XI

CORBY

"NINE out of ten's Scotch here," said the waitress at the Corby Hotel, making it sound as horrid as she could. "Well, you see," she added, to justify the exaggeration, "it's New Year's Eve tonight and they all get drunk." And finally she said, "Sort of Christmas for them, except they call it Hogmanay."

Christmas was long forgotten, and the crib in the new market square was already smashed. The balloons hanging in shop windows and blown up several weeks ago were now sagging, some soft and dimply and others quite deflated. The wine merchants still had queues of customers at ten o'clock, as the hours to midnight shortened, and people were slipping home with bottles in their pockets. In the Corby Candle, the only pub in the town centre, the men became more sentimental, talking about their daughters and their mothers and their bonnie Sco'land, and going through the war again. "I was a wee laddie . . ." The women became more giggly. Soon they would have to go through the ritual of the First Footing, carrying a lump of coal and a bottle of whisky to their neighbours; the parties would flicker on all over the town till dawn, like the remains of a forest fire. One might have been in Motherwell, or Coatbridge; and it was nice to remember that one wasn't.

"Everything's wee here," said the waitress grumpily. "There's no such word as small."

In the bar of the Hazel Tree, a modern pub in a housing estate called Beanfield, I found myself next to an Ulsterman. He had been a policeman in the colonial service and was now a security officer at the Corby steelworks. He was wearing his uniform trousers and heavy black boots, but had slipped on a tweed coat to come out to the pub. The barmaid, with a tiny pair of gold high-heeled shoes swinging from her ear-lobes, asked him if he was going to see the New Year in.

"Christ, no! They're just a lot of bloody savages. Mentioning no nationalities, of course. I've just spent ten years among people like that, and I don't want any more. I reckon Dr Banda would feel quite at home in Corby, never mind Nkrumah."

He talked about diamond smuggling down in the Union, and the price of wine in Lourenço Marques, and an adventure with a Siamese girl up in the Kra Isthmus. I suggested that Corby must be a bit dull after all that, but he liked it. He had a fine job, he had a cheap house, and best of all, he had a marvellous boss: "Never mind Churchill's bollocks, I'd tread on Prince Philip's bollocks sooner than on the general manager's. Even though he is a Scotsman."

He hated the Scots, and the trouble was, they made up more than half the population of Corby. They brought out the bagpipes at any excuse, he said, and they even had their bread and news-papers sent down from Glasgow—"never mind their haggis." The officer had gone into it all, almost obsessively. He said the Scotch church in Corby had the second biggest congregation in England, after Pont Street in London, and that during Glasgow Fair Week special trains and buses poured down from Scotland full of people who wanted to see how their relations in Corby were getting on; the trouble was, some of them never went back. Admittedly these were the dregs of Scotland, but it was a crying shame the steel company did so much of its recruiting up there.

Further along the bar were two middle-aged men who, by their faces and clothes and cigars, obviously were not Scotch. I had heard of the number of foreigners in Corby—Ukrainians, Aus-trians, Poles, Yugoslavs, Latvians—and I asked the officer if he knew what they were. He glanced round at them.

"Pure Aberdeen," he said in disgust. They were probably fisher-men. With the decline of the herring business lots of them had come to work in Corby; in some cases a skipper had sold his boat and brought his whole crew down to the steelworks. When they first came they had to live in an old army camp, and until they could be given a house by the Corby Development Corporation they usually left their families up in Scotland. They had to send money home, but with sixteen pounds a week or so there was still plenty left for clothes and hire purchase on cars and furniture—"never mind their beer." Six or seven pints a night, he said, was almost a rule. But even when their families joined them and they had lived several years in Corby they still talked about 'home' in

Scotland, though most of them never went back there. It was like Australians talking about England. There were children who had been born in Beanfield and had never crossed the border, but they talked as if they had never left the Glasgow slums.

"Take my kids," said a taxi-driver standing near us, who had been listening in. "They were born up there and were quite big when they left. They had never been away from their home in Glasgow before, but now they're nostalgic for the Scotland they never knew—for the banks and braes and all that." Two of his brothers and a cousin and several of his wife's relations had followed him to Corby, and the clan had hardly noticed that it had migrated, except that it was now much richer. They were going to have a rare time visiting each other after midnight. He was already getting maudlin, pouring down his pints of rotten English beer.

"You lot think the town belongs to you," said the officer. "Every night of the year, never mind New Year's Eve."

The Corby pubs are huge and quite un-memorable, like canteens. That night, my first in Corby and the last of 1963, I ended up in one within sight of the blast furnaces, on a seat with a frail English bachelor who told me his life story, edging nearer to me at the end of each chapter and sometimes hesitantly touching my arm. He'd had the first drink of his life in that very pub, but that was thirty years ago when it had a thatched roof and the town was like the Klondyke. He had just left school, a boarding school in Liverpool, after his parents, who owned a cinema, had lost everything in the slump and died without leaving him a penny. The old doorman they had employed wrote to him from Corby saying that there were jobs going in a new steelworks, and he had been in the company's office ever since. He was due for his gold watch in a few months. They got it automatically, after thirty years on the staff.

"Don't take any notice of him," said a Cockney sitting on the other side. "He's just an old male-bag." He caught me looking up at the photos of nudes pinned on the wall above our seat: "That's why he always sits in this corner. Gives it another twist, I suppose, with all those tits round his head."

The bar was packed full. There were people playing dominoes and darts, and young Scotch steelworkers smoking cigars with girls drinking Italian apéritifs. The divisions were not by class but by age-groups; one generation of men wore cloth caps and bicycle clips, another wore belted raincoats and trilbies, a third wore Beatle jackets and winkle-pickers. At a table in the middle were two thin boys in skin-tight jeans, with pale hunted faces and long cavalier ringlets, dirty copper-colour.

"The C.N.D. brigade," said the Cockney. "I bet there's many a girl'd like that hair." He told me about everybody. The three women in the party over in the opposite corner were tarts, and at the far end of the bar was the ton-up crowd, in leather jackets and crash helmets; one of them got killed every month, racing his bike on the motorway. And there was a Scotsman leaning across a table of domino-players, being hearty and buying everybody drinks; actually, he was very frightened, for he had been involved in a court case with another man who had been sent to prison, while he himself had got off; the other man was due out soon, and this fellow was getting worried. The Cockney said there was a lot of funny business like that in Corby. A few months ago a local businessman driving home from a party had knocked down a cyclist. In court the businessman had elected to go for trial, where the police as well as his own doctor had testified that he was drunk. But he had brought two barristers up from London to defend him, who had made mincemeat of the local witnesses, and he had been acquitted. Even he himself was said to have been surprised; and the cyclist was still in hospital.

"We're just waiting to see what happens the next time a poor bastard gets prosecuted, who can't afford a barrister from London," said the Cockney. "Of course, I've done time myself." And when I looked puzzled for a moment he added a little aggressively, "I say I've done time; been to prison."

Next morning Corby was an empty town, with a feeling of numbed unconsciousness everywhere. But by midday in the public bar of the Corby Hotel someone was singing 'Loch Lomond', and that night they were back again on 'I belong to Glasgie'.

During the next few days I learnt that in the public bars of Corby there was almost always somebody happy enough or lonely enough to begin singing. Sometimes it would be one man on his own, with a discreet and rather beautiful rendering of 'I'll walk beside you' and applauded by the women, or else two or three men trying to remember the words of 'Nellie Dean'. But as the waitress said, "Mostly they're Scotch here." And mostly it was a gang of happy steelworkers bawling about dear old Glasgie toun.

*   *   *

"Call George Joseph Brendan MacGugan!" shouted the police officer from the front bench of the court. A young man with a sad nervous face was shown into the dock. "Are you George Joseph Brendan MacGugan? Do you live at number ninety-three Bean-field Grove?" He was charged with breaking into his brother-in-law's house in the early hours of New Year's Day and stealing four pounds ten from the gas meter.

The brother-in-law, an even younger man who could hardly be more than twenty, stepped into the witness box. "Are you Bryce William Stewart, and do you live at eighteen Bessemer Avenue?" MacGugan smiled across the court at his brother-in-law, but Stewart kept a set face. He and his wife had left home at a quarter past midnight and gone to a party. They had made sure the windows and doors were fastened. They had returned at two o'clock. The lights in the house wouldn't work. After a few minutes they had gone out again to another party. They had come home finally at four-thirty and gone to bed in the dark. Next morning Stewart had found the cash box from the gas meter lying empty on the settee, and blood on the kitchen floor.

His evidence, taken down in longhand by the clerk of the court, was read back to him. A meter inspector from the gas board gave more evidence. A sheath knife was shown to the magistrates, who mumbled knowingly. The police officer read out MacGugan's statement on being charged: "I must have climbed over the back fence. I always had a key to the house. That's the knife I forced the meter with. I must have cut my hand. I was drunk when I did it. I can't remember anything about it."

The magistrates, under a carved coat-of-arms, mumbled again and committed him to the Northampton quarter sessions. The police officer said he would like custody, and MacGugan didn't protest. He was led away. Stewart and the meter inspector were bound over to appear at Northampton as witnesses, and each had to pay ten pounds to the clerk.

"Call Percy Terence Jamieson!" And the drunks, one after another, were put up in the dock and knocked down for forty shillings each.

*   *   *

Corby was difficult to grasp. Hopefully I drove round the countryside in the bare misty weather, and saw the farming land being torn up for the sake of the iron underneath the fields. The landscape, its wintriness enhanced by the spoliation, echoed with clanking ore trucks and sputtering diesel engines.

By night, when the mist had thinned, with a pale full moon gaping through the empty trees and the Great Bear hanging overhead, I came on a walking dragline, a beast of stupendous evil—the cousin of a dinosaur, or a multi-magnification of a praying mantis—sitting in a valley of mud in the middle of its own mess. Swiftly it swung its yellow neck from side to side and swivelled its hungry searchlights, biting up fifty-ton mouthfuls of England and spitting them out in mountains of chaos round itself. No noise came from its mouth, but a gentle electric whirring, perhaps from its stomach, hung in the vicinity. Every few minutes it lowered its big feet and ever so deliberately heaved itself a yard further forward.

By day I went inside it, and watched a man in an armchair controlling the devastation. I was in a machine of nearly two thousand tons, the size of a destroyer, with a crew of only two.

The feeling, at once of power and powerlessness, was the same in the steelworks, where giant saucepans of white-hot liquid were tipped casually into furnaces, where men sat up in glass boxes flicking levers and shunting logs of soft orange steel back and forth through the rollers, where strips were moulded into tubes, sparks shot screaming from the saws, magnets picked up tons of jangling pipes, where the only peace was in the building in which they kept the great mysterious computer, and where a Scotsman had fallen into the ore crushers on Christmas morning.

In the town centre there was a weird feeling of impermanence. It was odd to be in a place where there were no Georgian houses, however disfigured, no Gothic churches, no narrow High Street splitting with traffic. The Klondyke days may have passed, but they had been followed by an era that seemed hardly more substantial.

It was like being in the middle of a stage set, with the prop-builders still busy on the scenery. Nobody could tell how long the show would run, and because of the uncertainty or the lack of money or the disinterest of the influential people the promoters had hoped to attract, nobody was bothering very much. The toy-town decoration, the pointless patches of mosaic and bad sculpture, the silly balconies, the familiar slabs of blue and yellow, seemed no more solid than the tinfoil Christmas trees and paper streamers. Gorgeous Glasgow girls pushed the smartest pixie-dressed babies over muddy pavements in the most terrific prams, young men in mock sheepskins streamed out of the technical college into the bowling-alley, shadowy characters in jeans and donkey jackets hailed taxis and sped off to the far corners of nowhere—but at any time, one felt, the people might suddenly decide to go away, or be driven by some awful economic plague, and there would be nothing left but the monsters lying over the countryside and the havoc of thirty years' depredation; the sham would be blown away in the first strong wind.

Yet in a way it was refreshing that there was nothing beautiful in Corby to spoil, apart from the defaced land, and nothing abused to regret. Though the housing estates were interesting and sometimes attractive, the town centre was only an efficient machine for catering to the people, built for shopping in and for quickly forgetting. One would have minded the ugliness and the brisk impatience more if they had been at the expense of something lost; mercifully there had never been anything else. A placard in a fishmonger's heralded the beginning of 'Heat-and-Eat Week' in which pre-fried fish and chips that only needed warming up were being sold at knock-down prices; it was the consumer's lowest denominator—for if you wanted to consume a proper steak or a decent cup of coffee, let alone anything exotic like a new novel or a classical gramophone record, you had to go elsewhere, to Kettering or Northampton or Leicester—and it marked the epitome of Corby.

In search of a clue I went to church on Sunday morning, but it gave a barren answer. For a sermon the vicar told a story about a man who fell into a pit one dark night and couldn't get out. Some hours later a traveller passed by and the man shouted up to him for help. But it was only Confucius, who looked down and said, "You've made your bed, and now you must lie on it." He went on his way, and the man was left in the pit. Later, another traveller peered over the edge, and the man again called out for help. But it was Mohammed, who said, "Mysterious are the ways of Allah," and passed on. Then came Buddha, whose best advice was "Try meditation," and a Jew, who simply recommended a devout and good life. Finally there came a Christian; and the congregation gasped with appreciation.

At the door of the church, as I was going out, the vicar asked me round for a cup of tea, but I stammered something about only passing through, and slipped away. Corby was stranger and more arid even than I had thought.

*   *   *

When I asked a Scotsman in the steelworks about the foreigners, and if he knew any of them, he said, "Oh yes, I know a man in the coke-ovens. Comes from—what's that little country near Russia somewhere?" The impression was that, for all Corby cared about the little country, the man might never have left it; and it seemed too that the foreigners, for all they cared about Corby, had brought everything they could carry of their little country with them, and wanted nothing else.

There are five hundred Latvians in Corby, the biggest and proudest foreign community, and on midsummer's night they go out into the Northamptonshire woods and create a great Baltic forest full of songs and beer and bonfires and love-making, till dawn strikes the shadow of the steelworks and brings them sharply back to Corby. But even through the rest of the year they keep up the illusion. They have their own Latvian newspaper printed in London, and in their homes in the Corby housing estates they thumb happily through the pages of illustrated volumes of Latvian folklore. The women teach their children all the traditions, and some of them even scour Cornwall, Wales and Scotland for abstruse but comforting facts about the survival of minorities in Britain; and the men—'all professors, doctors and colonels' according to the Corby legend—tend to work as unskilled or semi-skilled workers in the dirtiest departments of the steelworks. They have no ambition—their ordeal has killed it all—except to preserve their culture; and to listen to them talking of their marvellous poets, their unequalled painters and their very famous politicians one realises the importance of their heritage, and one wonders why one has never heard of it before.

I sat at the back of a hall with a young Latvian and listened to hearty national carols being sung by the male voice choir, which for twenty years had sung its way through the refugee camps of Europe. The room was full of fat-faced men and blue-eyed women and little girls in plaits. A Lutheran priest stood up and in their language reminded them of the significance of Christmas at home and what it had meant to them in those distant Baltic winters; one day, I think he must have said, they would all go back and everything would be the same again. A lovely Christmas tree sparkling with white candles behind him suddenly caught fire, and a hefty baritone stepped forward to smother it.

The young man with me, who had been only a baby when his parents were driven from their country, had been educated at Corby grammar school; like so many Latvian children who seize on education as the only hope in an alien world, he had just spent three years reading mathematics at London University, and now he had returned to Corby with a job on the computer at the steelworks. But he didn't think he would stay long. Most of his friends had scattered to the big cities, or emigrated to America or Australia, and only one or two who had got degrees had come back to Corby. None of his generation really expected to see Latvia again, and anyway, the young man said, it would be a different place now. He had to think of his own future, not his people's past. The job on the computer was all right, and the company had promised him a career. But the trouble was Corby itself; it had no traditions.

*   *   *

Corby is a blot—a rootless, faceless, gormless blot. Thirty years ago, as they never cease telling you, it was a Northamptonshire village of twelve hundred people. "I've seen this place grow from nothing," they say, conscious of their history as people are who have only got the minimum, and proud enough to convince you that they did it all themselves. Nowadays it is the second biggest town in the county, with forty-five thousand people of nineteen different nationalities—or twenty-one, or twenty-six, depending on who tells you.

A few of those original twelve hundred must still be in Corby somewhere, just as a few sad old stone cottages can still be found, but they are smothered. Some ancient inscribed stones rescued from the demolished village have been inserted in the wall of the new public library, and I wouldn't be surprised to learn that some of the old villagers too have been preserved in the same way, cemented into one of the new buildings. The village of Corby has been buried in its own riches. The iron ore under the soil brought a steelworks, and the steelworks brought the people — the unemployed of England and the slum-dwellers of Scotland and the refugees of Europe. The village disappeared, with the fields and farms surrounding it, and a New Town appeared. New it certainly is; but it has yet to become a proper town.

"One-horseness is the word," said a clergyman. It was a company town, he said, built round the steelworks and as unbalanced socially as it was industrially. Thirty years ago, when the company first put up its steelworks, it built a workers' housing estate a few hundred yards from the blast furnaces and special staff houses for the managers in a park four miles away. Ever since, anybody who can afford it has tended to buy a house in one of the pretty stone villages of the neighbourhood, leaving the thousands of new houses in Corby to be occupied by the workers.

"It's soulless," said a bank manager. So far from being backward, he saw it as a town of the future, twenty-five years ahead of its time, and he found it a gloomy prospect. Apart from a few hairdressers and photographers, there was only a handful of private traders in the town; the rest of the shops were chain stores, with managers and little personality. It was a town built for a television audience, a town in which the garages went up before the houses, a town whose central pivot was a bus station.

"It's hopeless," said a publican who had lost forty dozen glasses stolen from his premises by customers on New Year's Eve and taken home for midnight parties.

"It's headless," said a man in the steelworks. Since it became designated as a New Town it had been controlled by a Development Corporation, a government-appointed body to which the people of Corby had no direct access. He acknowledged that it was necessary to have a Corporation, professionally organised and independent of local bickerings, to prepare and execute the plans for the town's development; but he regretted the autocratic methods, the supercilious attitude, and the fact that the chairman of the Corporation lived in Woking and that even the general manager preferred an old-fashioned village several miles from Corby. It hardly encouraged other professional and middle-class people to live in the town; it hardly encouraged the growth of self-respect; and it hardly encouraged people to take much interest in the Urban District Council, which waged a running fight with the Development Corporation but which attracted humdrum councillors and induced apathy among the electors. There were no patriarchs in Corby, no personalities and no prejudices; no one to worship, and no one to hate. One day they would come, but in a mushroom town that existed solely because of the expansion of one industry, it was too much to expect love and hope and pride and the thousand ingredients that make up a town's character — let alone its conflicts — to appear as quickly as the crescents and avenues of its housing estates.

"It's characterless," said a Scotsman. "You never know who you might find yourself living next to." He had had to ask the Corporation to move him and his family to another estate because across the road from his first house there had been a woman who never paid her grocer's bill but just took the grocer to bed, and he could never have his children brought up with that sort of thing going on.

"It's classless," said a Communist, adding that unfortunately it was classless for the wrong reason. But he was one of the few enthusiasts for Corby I met there, and the only constructive critic of the Corporation. He thought it was a scandal that the general manager of a body in charge of a town's development should be a civil engineer — as well as an absentee — and that there were no sociologists on the board; he blamed the Corporation for calling in London experts when often the expertise was on the doorstep; he resented the battles that had had to be fought for a maternity unit in the town, for co-education at the second grammar school when it had already worked so well at the first, and for the abolition of the eleven-plus. He mourned the few old cottages surviving from the original Corby village that were being demolished, and lamented the way Corby's opportunities were being squandered: "Take the grasshopper-warblers, for example. They don't nest in Hazel Wood any more. It's a tragedy." But all the same he liked living in Corby, and if, as they said, he was running a Communist cell there, I felt it could do nothing but good.

"It's shameless," said a man at the Corporation office, where they preserved a photograph of the huntsmen and hounds of the Woodland Pytchley moving off from a meet in Corby village thirty years ago, with the new blast furnaces rising in the background. But foxes, like grasshopper-warblers, are no longer found in the Corby woods, and the town's only substitute is ten-pin bowling; the Corporation tenants are not even allowed to keep pigeons. It was a town, the official felt, without loyalties and with no affinity with its neighbours. Though Kettering was only seven miles away — and though many Corby people went there to do their shopping, if only to escape from the impersonal chain stores — it belonged to no urban or industrial complex, and hardly even belonged to the county. It was a colony of strangers, disliked by Kettering for having already grown bigger and richer, and hated by rural Northamptonshire for having committed a nuisance — a disgusting, spreading mess — in the middle of their countryside.

Corby is blamed for everything in the district, and the people of Corby — prosperous, brash, with the lowest unemployment in the midlands and with hardly more interest in their town than in the surrounding country — just don't care. Apologists say that Corby's reputation was earned in the early days, when the steelworks and the first town buildings were being put up by contractors who brought in temporary labour that had nothing to lose by a bad name; or, "It's the birds of passage that cause all the trouble," they say, meaning the settlers who come to Corby but can't take it; and the local press, carefully making Corby the scapegoat for everything that goes wrong in the district, gives each Corby scandal individual treatment.

Certainly there is plenty of vandalism in Corby — window-breaking and wrecking of telephone boxes — but no more violence or serious crime than anywhere else, perhaps because there is so little hardship or distress. I was surprised that a heavy-industry town with an immigrant population from some of the toughest parts of Britain should cut such a mild figure, faceless and quite un-aggressive. 'Down with the Pope', chalked up to coincide with his trip to Israel, was the most outspoken thing I found; and probably it was only the Friday night effort of a member of the Corby Dauntless Few Loyal Orange Institution.

Corby is shapeless; geographically in that, although it doesn't sprawl like older towns, it is so loose-limbed that it has no articulate form; and socially in that, with a population that is unself-conscious and largely irresponsible, it has had no chance to develop a proper cohesion. Always there is the spirit behind the Corporation, 'them', a sort of impersonal Big Brother based in London, to whom Corby meekly surrenders; and it is this passive submission that makes the difference in the atmosphere between Corby and Kettering, for instance, the same as the difference between a supermarket and a private grocer. It is as if it had not yet been fertilised. Societies and committees, planted hopefully by a few keen people, blossom for a while but take no root and wither; and when a string quartet came to play, only fourteen people out of forty thousand turned up to listen.

"Corby's a eunuch," said a travelling salesman who was spending a few forlorn nights in the Corby Hotel. "Or rather I should say" — warming to the image — "it's still only a kid. Its voice hasn't cracked yet. Puberty will come, as it comes to us all one day." But he really wanted to talk about something else: "The best thing I ever did in all my life was install central heating." That was his favourite subject, followed by his daughter's education. "It isn't so important for a girl. So long as she's a good mixer, that's the thing. The social graces, you know." But he couldn't keep off central heating. "There's nothing like a warm bathroom." To kill the Corby winter evening he was learning Portuguese; one day he might go to Brazil, or he might retire to Portugal. "Very useful, Portuguese."

"I am eighteen and I have just spent the two most boring weeks of my life in Corby," was the beginning of a letter I read in the local paper. There was also a news item about two little Corby children who were always running away because they hated it so much, although they had only lived there a few months and had hardly given it a proper chance; this time they had been picked up on the road forty miles away, on the other side of Nottingham.

Yet Corby is a town of young people, where a funeral is a rarity and a grandmother almost unknown. It is all the more odd that there should be no Lyons Corner House, no Wimpy Bar, no fish and chip restaurant, in fact no restaurant open in the evening, only one gloomy coffee-bar, no dance hall, no cinema in the town centre, and no fun for anyone except in the bowling alley, where for a big price you can play the most boring game in the world. It will all come in time, they say, but between the passing of the grasshopper-warblers and the promised coming of the first Chinese restaurant there is only television, bingo, the betting shops and the pubs. Perhaps the eighteen-year-old letter-writer, like myself, somehow expected a New Town to engender a New Life, but it just isn't so. In the shops are the same mass-produced food, ugly clothes, furniture and jewellery as everywhere else; and through the windows on the housing estates — where people live in fine new houses among trees and grass and quiet, empty roads — one sees the same old curtains, the familiar wallpaper and lamp-shades and stained oak tables.

Everybody had something different to say about Corby, and yet although they contradicted each other I felt that all of them were right. It is a town of contrariness, a town where there are no natives and where nobody belongs, a town of outsiders, if it is a town at all.

XII

WISBECH

THE people of Cambridge would probably have been surprised early in January 1964 to be told that they had a Russian ship in their county; most of them possibly didn't even know they had a seaport. But in the far north, ten miles from the Wash, in a town that in its wilder moments calls itself 'the Gateway to the Industrial Midlands', an ancient coal-burning steamer flying the hammer and sickle and registered in Archangel was unloading two thousand tons of timber cut from somewhere beyond the Arctic Circle.

Actually, the old ship very nearly hadn't made it. The winter weather had given her a bad passage, extending it to twenty days; she had run out of coal, and for the last four days had had to break up her deck cargo and burn it for the boilers. But here she was, in the port of Wisbech, sharing it with a little Dutch coaster and the last of the old sailing-barges, a two-man vessel that came down every week from the Humber with a cargo of grain and carried it up the River Nene to Peterborough.

I asked the harbour-master if I could go aboard the Russian ship, in the vague hope of vodka with the captain, but he was not encouraging: "The captain will talk to me because we're both seafaring men, but I doubt if he'd have much to say to you. Anyway, there's a commissar on board, who would be suspicious." Instead, in his little fuggy office overlooking the stacks of timber on the quay, the harbour-master offered me a fill from his tobacco pouch and told me about his own days at sea; and in between the memories of hard tack and pound-and-pint and the old comradeship that no longer seemed to exist among seamen ("These days an apprentice wouldn't know a weevil if he met one") he got up and shouted out of the window to his stevedore to turn on the fresh-water pipe for the Russians and dispatched his pilot down the river to bring up another Dutchman.

The traffic at Wisbech amounts to two hundred ships a year,

but the harbour-master confessed that after all his years at sea, until he saw the advertisement for his job in the paper, he never knew it was a port at all. Now, however, he was restoring its old glory, and the Russian was the biggest ship that had yet come up the river.

"Of course," he said sadly, "if only the Ouse hadn't gone and changed its course we would be as important as King's Lynn." But centuries ago before the fens were drained, the big Ouse had shifted eastwards and left only the little Nene. "And of course if Britain had joined the Common Market we would have been laughing: we're the nearest east-coast port to Birmingham." But President de Gaulle had been as fickle as the Ouse.

To go from Corby to Wisbech was to return to a more familiar England. The handsome Georgian houses along the Brinks, over-looking the Nene, and the withered brick warehouses hanging over the mud at low tide were a comfort and a reassurance. There was nothing flimsy here. 'Capital of the Fens' was the proud notice at the borough boundary, and it didn't matter that somebody had altered it to 'Hospital of the Hens'. Wisbech could afford the little joke.

The town has an air of solid, historic respectability that Corby will never acquire, and although through the windows of the Georgian houses one now sees drainage engineers at their desks and accountants and fruit merchants and pretty girls at typewriters and cheesecake calendars on the walls, they impart such a feeling of prosperity that one is almost surprised the Wisbech elders are not even more boastful than they are. East Anglians, though they are proud and independent, are less aggressive about it than people from other parts; and for me it was a relief, after the con-fusion and elusiveness of Corby, to be back in a town where there was a recognisable pattern of continuity and evolution. Here were butchers' shops again, and cobblers, and a purveyor of seed potatoes to Her Majesty the Queen and a photographer 'patronised by Royalty', and a versatile merchant of metal and feathers and hair and skin. Life-size pictures of the Beatles were pasted over the windows of the music shop in the market square, but inside one could also buy a clarinet or the piano sonatas of Scarlatti. It's true there was bingo going on in the Corn Exchange, and even two Scotsmen on the pavement outside, wondering whether to go in; but they were commercial travellers, not settlers.

"Of course, this place is unique," said the first man I met in

Wisbech; and the second said, "Of course, I reckon there's nowhere else in the country quite like this." It was what people said wherever I went in England, and in a way they were right. No two places were the same, and it is a good thing that it should still be so. But if Wisbech has a parallel, it is with Bridgwater. Both are ancient ports up long tidal rivers, with old quays and granaries and rusting iron bollards; both have their lovely eighteenth-century buildings and their new industrial estates; both are market towns surrounded by low-lying fenland, rich with fruit and vegetables; both have jam factories and small engineering works; both have plans for developing the central shopping area, keeping traffic and pedestrians apart; and both have statues of their favourite heroes.

"Of course," said the clerk of the Wisbech and Marshland Rural District Council, a man who had originally come from the North Riding of Yorkshire, "they're a tight little community, these fen people. It takes a long time to get accepted." I remembered the town clerk of Bridgwater, who had come from Northumberland, talking about the devious ways of those men of Somerset and how long it had taken him to get accustomed to their strange, slow habits. But similarly the Yorkshireman had been won over to the fen country: "It's funny how it gets you. Lovely sunsets. Lots of sky." He was anxious not to give the impression he didn't like the fen people: "Of course, they're a bit slow off the mark. Let me put it like this—they're soccer players rather than rugger players."

"Of course," said the mayor, "you know we've all got webbed feet here." I sat drinking municipal whisky in his parlour, surrounded by civic dignitaries and pictures of past mayors, while his worship, with gin and a cigar, told me about their plans for developing the town, and for signing a twin-town alliance with Arles in the Rhône valley; I remembered that Bridgwater also had a twin in the south of France. The mayor only hoped that the ceremony could be performed while he was still in office, so that he could carry the greetings of Wisbech to Arles himself.

"Of course," said the deputy town clerk, "I don't expect we shall go in for bull-fighting and that sort of thing."

"Of course," said the town clerk, "I suppose you know we have the best strawberries in England. The Kent ones may ripen a week or so earlier, but they're nothing like ours."

"Of course," said the deputy town clerk, "we've got a very fine operatic society."

"Of course," said the deputy mayor, "you know all about King John losing his crown in the Wash, don't you?"

"Of course," said I, learning the language, "the only English Pope came from somewhere near here, didn't he?" But nobody seemed to know about that, and somebody mumbled something about a strong puritan tradition: "Of course, you'll soon be knowing more about Wisbech than we do ourselves."

But they had their worries, and one of them was the hundreds of young men who had taken to driving twenty miles every morning to work in the big engineering factory at Peterborough. Many of them had had four or five acres of fenland which they had sold or rented, because they had become uneconomic to farm; and as soon as they could find homes in Peterborough near their new work they would be lost to Wisbech.

"It tells on their health," said the local secretary of the farmers' union, in his office under a picture of a luscious nude. "They miss the fresh air in that factory, though of course they get good money there." Not that any of the fen farmers are doing badly, he said, but there was a tendency for the smallest plots to get absorbed, which was not surprising when the price was three hundred pounds or more an acre, though half the land in his area was still divided into farms of under fifty acres, and most of them were between ten and twenty.

"It's different up in the highlands," and he pointed with his cigar in the direction of the nude; when I looked surprised he added, "I mean, up in Norfolk." Very intensive, he called the farming round Wisbech, and very independent the farmers, probably because there had never been any big landowners in the district. There was nothing like the fens in the world, except in Holland, and frequently the secretary went over there to compare problems of land reclamation and drainage and growing bulbs, and to bring back another supply of Dutch cigars.

Holland is everywhere about Wisbech, in the cigar smoke of its borough offices as in every aspect of the countryside. There are old Wisbech families with old Dutch names, and one doesn't have to drive far across the flat, fat land before reaching a notice, 'County of South Holland'.

Another roadside notice says, 'Please dip headlights as ships approach', which might be surprising in a region less weird; but in the fenland one is as likely to come across a cargo ship sailing high above the fields of sugar beet as on a pretty brick farmhouse standing guard, with a black shed and a monkey-puzzle tree, over three acres of strawberries.

Perhaps it was at its best in January, when the soil, rich and moist like Christmas pudding, had just been ploughed, when the dark clamps and canal banks were flecked with frost, and when the fields were not yet covered with the drab green of potato haulms and turnip tops. The land is anti-picturesque; its beauty is in the colour of the earth and the light behind the winter trees, and in the feeling one gets of standing on an endless misty world in which a valley or a hill would be absurd. One gets another feeling too, of helplessness, from the straight rivers carried on high embankments across the land and from the hidden sea behind its dyke. And at night, so flat is everything around that it is as if the sea has stealthily come in and the lights of villages and farms are ships.

"Of course," said a man who managed the affairs of fourteen different drainage boards financed by farms drained by the River Nene, "they've each got their own separate Act of Parliament, some of them going back to the sixteen hundreds."

"These farmers!" said the landlord of Ye Olde George. "They are too darned rich. There's one who comes in here every night. He won forty-five thousand quid on the pools, and gave it all to charity. I ask you! He's called Fred. He'll be in later. I'll call him Fred so you can see which he is."

The customers in the public bar were mostly youths with half pints of bitter and girls with goblets of grapefruit juice. But they varied from pub to pub, and in the Mermaid, on the same side of the market square, there were big weather-beaten men with pints of brown-and-mild playing dominoes for money and only one or two women waiting for their husbands. And in the Ship, further along, there was a sleek Chinese ordering a whisky and lemonade for himself and a rum and blackcurrant juice for his shaggy long-haired friend. I talked to a sad fat man at the bar who drank pints of bitter and told me about his life as a conjurer at children's parties, a bingo-caller for old-age pensioners, master of ceremonies at club dances, and general entertainer at the pickers' camps during the strawberry season.

"That's my busy time," he said, "apart from Christmas and the New Year."

"Don't you believe a word," said his wife, sitting alone at a table behind him, with a gin and tonic. "He works at the Co-op." But he went on talking about the campers and the gipsies and the diddicoys, while I bought him more bitter, until his wife got up and took him away, leaving me wondering about the diddicoys.

In the Rose and Crown, across the square, the commercial travellers tried to outdo each other in motor accidents, capping each smash with a bigger one.

"You remember David? You know he was killed on Boxing Day, don't you? He'd only been married three weeks. On a level crossing. Some runaway trucks they were shunting. He couldn't have been more than twenty-six. You know, David the Scotch fellow. With a beard, a wispy beard round his chin. To look at, you'd think he was a Frenchman, until he opened his big Scotch mouth."

"Some friends of my wife's. A couple, with a tiny baby in the back of the car. In a Zodiac. They drove right through this brick wall into a cemetery. Might as well have left them there, really. They were taken to hospital, but it wasn't any good. But the baby was all right, except it never learnt to talk. Funny thing, that. It must be about four now, and still can't talk."

"Well, outside Norwich last week I saw this Mini underneath a big eight-wheeler. Right underneath, between the wheels. The truck was just sitting on it, like an old hen sitting on an egg. But of course, the egg was smashed. Completely. Very nasty, I should think."

"That pile-up on the motorway last night, in the fog. Two hundred cars in one smash. Fantastic. Christ though, I'd have given anything to see it afterwards."

Upstairs in the restaurant a peppery old man in a cavalry waistcoat, just finishing his dinner and watching the young waiter pouring out his coffee, treated him to a lesson: "There are two sorts of brandy. There's a Cognac. And there's an Armagnac. But I don't suppose you'd know about that. I don't suppose you'd have an Armagnac here. I'll have a Curaçao."

When the pubs shut at night the young men come out into the market square with their girls, get into their cars, race the engines for a minute, roar round the square a couple of times gathering speed, and shoot off down a side street into the fens.

"Of course," said a man who had built up an engineering firm from a small beginning in a shed on his father's farm, "three years ago this was an orchard"—and I found it hard not to tell him I wished it still was. The orchard was now a factory employing a hundred men to make special lorry bodies, with a branch factory in Belgium set up in anticipation of the Common Market.

But even though Wisbech wants more factories like that, there is no danger of the town or its surroundings getting badly spoilt. Whereas Corby depends on iron ore dug from the soil, nothing could ever be dug out of the fens, except possibly King John's treasure. The wild cranes and bitterns have gone, debts are no longer paid in eels, and woad hasn't been cultivated for some years now; but the men who fought the battle of the fens—the Romans and the Earl of Bedford with his Gentlemen Adventurers and the imported Dutchmen and the little bog-dwellers themselves—created the richest farming land in England, and it is unlikely that anyone will ever want to turn it into anything else. And Wisbech itself, like the pumps and sluices of the countryside, gives the impression of belonging to a system perfected over the years, in which each function fits inevitably into the pattern.

It isn't just that the canning factories will go on buying fruit and vegetables as long as the farmers go on growing them; but the organist in the parish church will go on playing Bach jigs on winter Saturday afternoons as long as the pubs are open all day on market day, the church bells will play the 'Men of Harlech' early on Sunday mornings as long as the Salvation Army band takes over the empty market square on Sunday evenings, and the people of Wisbech will go on taking their holidays in Hunstanton, where the sun rises perversely over Norfolk and sets over the sea, as long as the wrestling tournament pays its monthly visit to the Corn Exchange.

"Of course," said I to the man next to me at the ringside, "it's all fixed beforehand."

"Yes and no," he replied. "It's showmanship, certainly; and they want to make it exciting so that the people will come and watch them again next month. But it's a rough game."

We sat under the Victorian cast-iron and glass roof of the Corn Exchange. "I wanna hold your hand," yelled the Beatles from loudspeakers somewhere up among the coloured lights. A huge fish-net hung above us, on the walls were advertisements for roller-skating lessons, and a smell of fried onions drifted over the crowd from the hot-dog stand in the corner. Children with autograph books thrust them in the face of anyone who looked like a wrestler. Nobody thrust anything at me. "Didn't think much of the Beatles last night, did you?" said a kid behind me to his chum, and as if he had been overheard the loudspeakers suddenly switched into Macnamara's Band.

"Let's get started!" shouted a man after the first pair of wrestlers had been bear-acting for a round and a half. They groaned and slapped each other's flesh and thumped the floor.

"That didn't hurt you!" jeered a woman's voice when one of the fighters gasped with pain; she stood up by the ring and shook her fist through the ropes at him.

"Shut your big mouth!" bellowed the wrestler.

"Chicken!" screamed somebody.

"That's the sort of bloke I like," said my neighbour, when a pair of heavyweights took the ring, one of them a grizzly brute with a ferocious scowl. "He's dangerous." But he was hated by the people of Wisbech, and though he was much better than his opponent he was constantly booed. "To be at the top, I reckon you've got to be either very popular or very unpopular. Which-ever way, you'll always draw a crowd."

"He don't want to marry you!" shouted somebody when the wrestlers were locked together like dogs.

"What do you know about it?" asked the brute, looking between his opponent's legs and sticking his own massive bottom through the ropes.

"That'll put your piles back!"

The brute won, as he was expected to, but only after a lot of fuss and anguish. The crowd yelled at him and he smirked trium-phantly. More fights followed, the result as inevitable as in a bull-ring, the spectacle no more interesting than the ten-pin bowling at Corby; the bodies were ugly, and the excitement negligible. But it pleased Wisbech.

Afterwards, outside the Corn Exchange, I saw the loser of the last fight, an Argentinian who had surrendered after a terrible mangling, walk calmly across the road to his Jaguar and drive away. With his brief-case and wide overcoat, and without his

5*

little black moustache, he might have been a successful strawberry farmer or a drainage contractor, or even an officer from the Russian steamer in the river.

I went into a pub along the river, where the crowd was arguing about bostons and half-nelsons, and the master of ceremonies, a failed actor in a stained dinner jacket, was standing drinks all round. A young man sitting alone at the bar took no notice of the others, and peered dreamily into his beer.

"Of course," said the barmaid, "this lad's going off to the land of sunshine next week. Emigrating to Australia. Some people get all the luck." And he smiled dimly.

XIII

CHERTSEY

I was swept up the escalator from the underground and deposited in the middle of Waterloo station. The relentlessness of the operation was made still more bewildering by the composure of the rush-hour crowd. It would have been impossible to stop or turn back or even pull out a handkerchief and blow one's nose, and yet there was none of the hubbub, let alone panic, that traditionally goes with a crowd of people on the move. There was no talking or shouting or laughing or weeping, no excitement or terror, no sticks and stones or bodies trampled underfoot. It was just the routine exodus of a mass of English men and women who had arrived in London that morning and were now going home; they did it every weekday, every week, all through their lives. For them each minute of the journey was scheduled, each footstep marked. Without the silent pressure of the crowd and the swift yet unfrenzied motion through tunnels and up escalators they might individually have been lost.

Opposite the top of the escalator, across the crowded platform, I saw the suburban booking office. All the windows except two were shut. It seemed incredible, in the rush-hour, but I supposed that everyone had season tickets. I joined one of the queues. Up under the glass roof of the station somebody was playing a saxophone, many years ago. There was a predominant noise of feet everywhere and something else indefinable – pigeons? taxi-engines idling? tired breathing? The huge four-faced clock, Gothic and imperial, hanging over the station was jerking out the minutes. Five-sixteen. Five-seventeen. I had once met a girl under that clock, long ago, but now I couldn't even remember her name. We had both been so bored. We had gone to a cinema and afterwards I had ungallantly taken her to the entrance of Piccadilly Circus underground station and asked her if she could find her own way home. Five-eighteen. Over the window at the head of the queue it said, 'Book here for Addlestone.' I had never heard of it, and couldn't visualise it. Beautiful Addlestone, Addlestone beside the Thames, Addlestone among the pines—nothing quite fitted. Book here for Addlestone, Aldershot, Ascot, Ashtead, Bagshot, Balham, Banstead. Recognition glimmered; I was beginning to see the rows of red roofs. Barnes, Barnes Bridge. But that was in London, not the suburbs, and I had lived there once. Ridiculous; I couldn't possibly go there; I might meet someone I knew. Beckenham. I had been to a factory there once—a tannery where they made very expensive leather; but I couldn't remember anything except the heaps of crocodile skins and pig skins, and hoping for a present of an ostrich skin. Belmont, Berrylands, Birkbeck, Bookham, Bracknell, Brookwood, Byfleet. It was like a Betjeman poem, written up in white capitals on a green board. The queue moved forward, but I still hadn't decided where to go. The clock jerked again; five-twenty. Camberley, Carshalton, Cheam, Chessington, Chertsey . . . I was at the window.

"Single to Chertsey," I said boldly. It sounded as good as any of the others.

"Which way?" said a voice through the glass. I hadn't bargained for that.

"Which way have you got?"

"Staines or Weybridge?"

"What's the difference?" I asked. There was more to this commuting than I had thought.

"Staines direct, Weybridge cheaper." He sounded impatient. People in the queue behind me began to mutter.

"Weybridge," I said, pushing a ten-shilling note through the window, taking the ticket and hurrying away as if I knew which platform to go to for the Chertsey trains. Five-twenty-two.

"Your change!" shouted about six people at once, and the whole queue turned and looked at me with pity.

I found an indicator giving the platforms of trains. Five-twenty-three. There was a five-twenty-four to Chertsey via Staines from platform seventeen. I could always pay the extra. It was a long way through the crowd, but I wasn't going to run. Nobody else was running, except a young man with a beard who didn't look like a real commuter anyway. At a stall there was a bunch of men calmly drinking cups of scalding tea, who couldn't possibly have been going anywhere but Chertsey by the five-twenty-four; they had it written all over them; we still had a full minute, though one can never tell with clocks that jerk. I reached platform seventeen just as they shut the gates, just as the clock jerked.

"Four out of five top civil servants take *The Times*," said a poster over the platform. Perhaps I should have booked for Addlestone instead.

I went back to the platform indicator and found another train to Chertsey via Staines at five-thirty-seven from platform twenty. I asked a man about Weybridge. He said there was another indicator for the Weybridge line at the far end of Waterloo. Five-twenty-five. I went there, through the crowd. It was like swimming — not through calm water or a steady stream, but through the turbulent water below a weir where currents come from all directions; I kept on hitting rocks. Five-twenty-six. There was a train to Chertsey via Weybridge at five-twenty-seven from platform thirteen. I went there, through the crowd. I passed the tea stall again, where the men were still calmly sipping hot tea, but now they were different men; the first lot must have caught the five-twenty-four. I reached platform thirteen just as they shut the gates, just as the clock jerked.

"Three-quarters of top businessmen take *The Times*," said a poster over the platform.

I was beginning to lose my temper. Commuting was more complicated than I had imagined. But nobody else was bad-tempered and they had all done it yesterday and the day before, and in the morning too, and had spent the day in an office. I had had tea at home. Five-twenty-nine. I went back through the crowd to the second platform indicator. There was a train to Chertsey via Weybridge at five-forty-seven from platform thirteen, where I had just come from, but that meant nearly twenty minutes to wait. Then I remembered that on the first indicator there had been a train via Staines at five-thirty-seven, but I couldn't remember the platform. So I went back through the crowd to look. Platform twenty. The clock jerked; five-thirty-one. At the tea stall there was yet another bunch of men; the second lot must have caught the five-twenty-seven. But perhaps they were all going to Addlestone, not Chertsey. The thought of Addlestone kept cropping up.

I reached platform twenty with five minutes to spare and confidently flourished my ticket to the collector as I went through the gate. Without looking at me he pushed it back into my chest and said, "Weybridge five-forty-seven platform thirteen." I felt too dizzy to argue.

"Two-thirds of top authors take *The Times*," said a poster over the platform.

The rush-hour was at its peak, the station entrances were spewing out people like a jack-pot, the platforms were swallowing them whole, the trains were rolling out to Addlestone, Bagshot, Byfleet, Chertsey. I tried to savour the commotion, but I felt too angry at having missed three trains in thirteen minutes. The men at the tea stall, still calmly sipping their hot tea, had changed again; all the others must now be hurtling through the suburbs. The saxophone went on playing and the clock jerking. Five-thirty-eight.

I caught the five-forty-seven, nearly half an hour after buying my ticket. I got a seat in a long carriage with an aisle down the middle, full of pipe smoke and the smell of fresh newspapers. Late-comers who couldn't find seats grunted, put their bowlers and brief-cases on the rack, opened their evening papers and grunted again. Two women had to stand, because nobody offered them seats. Nobody spoke. The train started, and the middle-aged man in a green suit next to me, reading a textbook on quantum mechanics, checked the time on his watch. A young man had a magazine about cars, a girl had a magazine about houses; but most people had evening papers.

"ALL WELL" was the front headline of the *Evening News*.

"VERY WELL" was the front headline of the *Evening Standard*. The Queen Mother had had her appendix out that morning.

We rocked past London's clock towers and advertisements for gin, into the suburban night; through the bingo country, out into the Green Shield belt. Nobody looked out of the train; the windows were soon steamed up with smoke and warm breath. At Surbiton people got out, and the rest of us adjusted ourselves and sighed. At Esher a woman who had been asleep in the corner opened a paper bag, took out an unfinished green jersey, knitted one row, put it away again, got out when the train stopped without looking to see the name of the station. Between Weybridge and Chertsey the carriage was almost empty; looking at the bare seats it was hard to remember what it had been like at the beginning. All those men were already walking home, or stopping at a pub, or kissing their wives; the girls were shopping

for their suppers. The last station before Chertsey was called
Addlestone, written up in white capitals on a green board.

*   *   *

At the pub where I stayed the decorators were in and the heating was off. There was a bottle of milk in the bath, and teacups
and muzak everywhere, and china ducks in flight across the
cream embossed wallpaper. In the lounge bar were lithographs by
John Piper and a frieze made of the tips of club ties pinned to a
shelf of miniature liqueur bottles—Esher Rugger Club, Surrey
Amateur Boxing Association, Royal Singapore Service Club,
Whitgift School tucked in among the tiny Green Chartreuses and
Cherry Heerings. An immense dog, vaguely Pyrenean, dirty and
fat from years of sniffing beer, lay on the floor behind the bar.
The barman, a man of fifty in a grey cardigan, with a small
moustache and a public school voice, made me think of an army
officer cashiered for embezzling the mess funds. The customers
called him Norm. He offered me a cigarette.

"Smoke, sir?"

"No, I don't, thanks."

"Lucky man." He said something about his lady nicotine. The
conversation turned to cars, and a man offered the information
that clergymen were a special insurance risk, and brokers would
only take them on at a higher premium.

"All that sly drinking, I suppose," said Norm. "You know, a
glass of wine every day before breakfast." Over the fireplace was
a machine for testing your drunkenness; you set the dials to the
amount you had drunk, your weight and your sex, put in sixpence
and it showed the amount of alcohol in your blood. The manu-
facturers, it said, took no responsibility.

How was the new car? Going like a bomb. How was the new
dog? Settling down nicely. How was Doreen? She was on a
diet.

"Do I smell bangers?" said a man breezily, just off the train
from Waterloo. Norm said No, and praised the Spanish staff:
"Very good team we've got now. But they have their drawbacks,
you know. Not too hot on the lingo and that. You ask for
poached eggs and you get them scrambled. But they're willing.
Too willing sometimes. They pretend they understand more than
they do."

I saw what he meant in the dining-room, at supper. The Spanish waiter got in a disastrous muddle and packed up completely when the only other customer, an Englishman with two weeks' experience on the Costa Brava behind him, said, "*Qué nacionalidad?*" When the waiter looked dumb the Englishman repeated it a little faster and a little louder, and then a third time. Norm came to the rescue and served us soup that tasted of mushroom and asparagus at alternate mouthfuls, and mixed grill. "Sorry, sir, we've been trying to find some rolls, but all we've got is this sliced bread." The Spanish team in the kitchen was doing its best, despite the lingo, but with the ice-cream Norm's pretence at efficiency collapsed: "The dancing girls will be on very shortly." I hadn't realised till then that I was expecting them.

Back in the lounge somebody had brought in an old dog with a hump on its back like an Indian ox. It could hardly hobble, and fell on the floor beside its owner.

"Poor old chap," said a man. "What's the trouble. Growth?"

"Yes. I've watched it grow. It's been coming on for two years. The vet says it won't be long now."

"Isn't he lovely and docile?" said a woman. The dog couldn't move.

"What's the Spanish for cold, old man? *Caliente?* Thanks, I must remember that. *Caliente.*"

"Funny, I always thought that was hot."

Norm told me about Chertsey. The trouble, he said, was that people never came to Chertsey on purpose. "Chertsey?" they said, when he told them where he lived. "Let's see; that must be on the way to Virginia Water, isn't it?" Or, "You go through it on the road from Staines to Weybridge, don't you?" Once, years ago, a film star from the studios at Shepperton across the river had been brought over to Chertsey to see a doctor; but that was the only occasion Norm could remember.

"I despise the Americans," said an intense woman in trousers. "They've brought every *vice* to this country." She uttered the word *vice* as though she had learnt to pronounce it at a drama school, from deep down in her throat. A poodle barked outside the door, and she went to let it in.

A man said, "Twenty-seven holes at Sunningdale would suit me fine tomorrow, if the weather's like it was today. Eighteen in the morning, then a few beers, and nine in the afternoon." He was a man with technical knowledge of many things; he talked of the air-frost, and of a plastic bathroom mirror that didn't steam up, and of lung cancer, as well as of cars and dogs. But nobody I met in Chertsey talked about politics, and when I mentioned the coming general election there was silence and a few looks of derision.

In the public bar, however, the atmosphere was more homely and the people more practical. There was a generous barmaid who laughed at her own jokes; and young engineers in blazers from the aircraft factory, exiles in Surrey, with their home-town local newspapers stuck in their pockets; there was the same talk of cars, but of hire-purchase rather than dogs; there was a woman whose small daughter was teaching her the twist; and there were people washed up on the shores of suburban society, drinking stout and milk, or lager and lime, or whisky and orange, or rum and blackcurrant.

"Mick? He's all right. But . . . Mick can be very, very nasty."

"Mick? He wouldn't pull a black man off his grandmother. But . . . as you say, Mick's all right."

A woman said, "Come on, girls, let's play the men!" She chalked up their names beside the dart board—Glad, Phyl, Madge and Elaine against Stan, Eddy, Don and Smiff—smart, hard women against smart, soft men. They played darts beautifully.

* * *

Nobody could say of Chertsey that it is unique, or that there is nothing else like it in England. Most of its neighbours—Weybridge or Woking, Egham or Esher, Cobham or Chobham—are hardly different, and the species extends in a throttling circle round London. The Green Line buses that snort through Chertsey on their way to Gravesend and Welwyn Garden City, on the opposite side of the great wen, testify to the conspiracy of the suburbs. There are no rivalries, and very few identities. They are not market towns or industrial towns or holiday towns, but huge residential hotels, with hundreds of commuters' cars parked all day outside the railway stations, like shoes outside the bedroom doors.

In the early morning the cars tear through the laburnum groves and acacia avenues to the station yard, and men hurry under the pine trees and across the patches of heath, panting in the cold winter air. But after the first rush there is an hour or two of emptiness, except for milkmen and window-cleaners, until the women come out to do their shopping. During that gentle morning lull, when the Thames mist scatters and the pale sun shines through the little lost groves of silver birches, it is not hard to remember that England's biggest cemetery is just a few miles away.

The most important shops are the ones that sell cars, and the next in importance are the petrol stations. But this is not a particularly new phenomenon, for ever since the racing days at Brooklands there has been a tradition of motoring in the district; this is Lagonda country, and vintage sports cars are still driven slowly, like tired old ghosts, along the by-passes.

It is also a district, if one is to believe the guide-book, famous for its highwaymen, and they do their best to preserve the memory of bygone Surrey. Packhorse Inns crouch among the convents, antique shops outnumber the Home and Colonial Stores, and little old brick houses smile from behind the war memorials. But the garages win hands down, and on the whole the occasional Georgian fanlight or Venetian window or Regency porch is as irrelevant as the notices about keeping horses and cattle off the grass verges. Somewhere hidden behind the tall poplars is the Thames, and three men in a boat, and an island where the Magna Carta was signed; but the tall poplars too are hidden by advertisements for Shell Super.

Almost as prosperous as the motor trade, as fits a residential place, is the estate agents' business; their offices thrive in every High Street, sandwiched between Jennifer who sells china dogs and Pollyanna who sells home-made fudge. Property is a commodity as vital as toasted tea-cakes, and testimony to its value is seen in the gaps torn out of high cypress hedges to reveal raw new flats and houses. The great spreading parks were bitten into first, and now it is the gardens of the big villas; development was not enough, but super-development had to come, and the old order of those halcyon Betjeman days is gone.

In the High Street cafés women in purple hats sit like beleaguered dowagers, gossiping over tea and scones, attended by sharp-voiced waitresses who have seen better days and like to take it out of their customers: "I haven't got any meringues left;

you're much too late for those." The customers rather like it too, and they slip threepenny bits under their saucers and hurry out. The greyer ladies, widowed and well-off, retire behind the cedar trees of park hotels, muffled and unlicensed and once private mansions, where they take their tea increasingly silently beneath the antlered trophies of former owners. At weekends their nephews visit them, and escape after tea to the squash courts and miniature golf course and to unkind thoughts.

"Let's go with Labour!" on a poster in the middle of Chertsey was an anomaly; across the street Sir Alec Home's watery eyes and mild smile were more appropriate. The only cinema was shut, a post office and a supermarket had also closed down, and the offices of the Urban Distict Council had been transferred—to Addlestone. Dancing lessons and violin tuition were advertised in a newsagent's; someone had lost a cat, and someone else a budgerigar, "very friendly, lands on finger, answers to wolf whistle"; pullets were for sale, puppies were to be given away to good homes, friendship or marriage was offered, and Christ died for the ungodly.

Sometimes an astonished swan flies high over Chertsey's red roofs; and if one walks down Colonel's Lane, past the semi-detached houses of Abbey Gardens where thirteen centuries ago Erkenwald was abbot, past Saint Anne's Hill where Iron Age Britons and Charles James Fox once lived, across Laleham golf course where the players still arrive by punt across the Thames, one comes to a field of green corn, and even a few sheep. The houses are closing in on them fast—worldly like Greenacres, well-travelled like Grindelwald, coy like Kumincyde—and each year a few more acres are nibbled by the gravel pits and caravan estates. But despite the old cars rotting in the woods, despite the motor launches tarpaulined for the winter, despite Bung-ho, the super caravan in a meadow with plastic gladioli in its windows and concrete gnomes in its garden, a few farmers still sow crops in the Surrey soil, and a few swans breed.

There was one feature of modern England that I missed—the leavening of coloured immigrants—until one night, walking over a heath under the frosty February stars I met a black girl hurrying towards me, her high heels clipping and tripping in the dark, her hot African breath blowing into the night.

"Mister please, is way to Weybridge?" She went clipping on

down the hill, beautiful under Orion, leaving me watching her and wishing.

*   *   *

In the morning I caught the commuters' train back to Waterloo. At Addlestone I opened the door for a woman who was getting in, and both she and the other passengers gave me the sort of look ("Poor chap, he doesn't know the form") that I had come to expect. At Weybridge, where we had to change, there were rows of black figures stamping up and down the platform, blind to the faces they encountered every day; even an eccentric who had put on a Russian fur hat in deference to the weather was ignored.

"What makes the trains go so bad when it's cold, I wonder?" said a testy man to the ticket-collector, but he didn't really expect an answer.

When the train came we crowded in, slammed the doors and pounced on the first seat we could find. In my carriage was the familiar smell of pipe-smoke and newspapers — *Telegraphs, Expresses, Mails, Woking Heralds,* and one top *Times,* a golden-haired girl in a fur hat and high boots, only slightly spoilt by hasty face-powder.

Nobody looked out at the sharp winter sun shining on the frosty playing fields, on the allotments and back gardens and unknown rivers and gravel pits and waterworks and private schools for boys and girls; the lovely morning was wasted, and slowly the steam thickened on the windows so that it didn't matter.

At Waterloo, instead of a saxophone, an invisible military band under the roof was playing 'the Fairest of the Fair'. The crowds slipped like bath-water down into the underground, back to the office. I caught sight of a negro sitting on a bench with two hats on his head, and went home to breakfast.

XIV

OCKBROOK

ALL day long the noise of traffic rolls past Ockbrook vicarage, along the four-lane concrete by-pass between Derby and Nottingham that neatly splits the parish and brings peril to anybody trying to get from All Saints' to Saint Stephen's. Too often, through the hedge and across the overgrown garden, comes the familiar scream of rubber and crash-tinkle-tinkle; and too often the doctor who lives on the other corner is called out to attend to the damage. I hadn't been at the vicarage half an hour before we heard a smash, and the vicar, still clutching his baby daughter, ran out to investigate; it was a small local van in collision with a big new Rover, and nobody was hurt; but the death roll at that cross-roads steadily rises, and may yet catch up with the death roll on the war memorial opposite the vicarage gate.

"One of the puppies has got its eyes open!" shouted the vicar's wife joyfully out of the kitchen window, as the vicar and I dug up the drive and tried to unblock the vicarage drains. She was looking after three small daughters and two white cats and a labrador bitch with five puppies, and she was making marmalade and sending a card to a sick parishioner and telephoning the vet and soothing the baby after a whooping-cough injection and hanging up nappies and fetching eggs from across the road and cooking the lunch.

The vet came, a tough Scotsman in a car deep in empty Woodbine packets, with manure on his trousers. He lanced an abscess behind a puppy's ear, and as he pressed out the pus he told us how his fingers tingled for work. If he was on top of a bus and the man in front had a big blackhead on the back of his neck, he could hardly restrain himself from leaning forward and squeezing it out. I felt uneasy until he had driven away.

A lugubrious grave-digger turned up on a bicycle and looked gloomily at the drains without getting off; at last we cleared the blockage, and though the smell of sewage lingered the vicar was soon gone. He was almost always gone, on the business of his seven thousand parishioners, even when he hadn't got a service at one of his two churches: gone to a confirmation class, gone to visit a widow in her cottage, gone to see an old man in Derby hospital, gone to pick up a daughter from school, gone to see the organist about a wedding, gone to see a school-teacher about the parish magazine, gone to see the Roman Catholic priest about a lecture on Christian unity, gone to the diocesan house, gone to the old people's home, gone to the approved school, gone to fetch me from the station. He could hardly stop to think, except during the anxious minutes when he was trying to cross the traffic on the by-pass.

"Two funerals, and the morning's gone." Even on Monday morning, the day he tried to keep free from parish work, he had a funeral, which exasperated his wife; the undertaker didn't work all Sunday like the vicar, and even the crematorium had changed to a five-day week.

"Ah, but it's old George," said the vicar, "and he's been dead over a week already." But his wife didn't see why George couldn't wait another day; her husband's over-work was more worrying than the children and dogs and cats.

"Meetings, meetings, meetings," she said. "And at the end of each meeting do you know what they do? They decide to have another meeting." It sounded like a voice from Jane Austen, until we switched on the television from Miami Beach and watched Cassius Clay knock out Sonny Liston to become heavyweight champion of the world. Nothing was too exotic for Ockbrook vicarage. And nothing was too much trouble for the vicar, though he would have liked a little more time for his work towards uniting the four Christian denominations in Ockbrook; it wasn't the different clergymen that put up obstacles so much as the ignorance, making for prejudice and suspicion, of their congregations.

Across the road an old man with gory razor cuts between the tufts of white hair on his face and with a grey Homburg that looked as if it hadn't been lifted for years, was shuffling round his garden on two sticks. He was a Methodist himself, and he said it as a housewife might say she shopped at Sainsbury's rather than at the Co-op, because the service was better. He had been born in the seventies of last century, not in Ockbrook but up in Stafford-

shire, six miles from Leek. He didn't expect I knew Leek, but it
was up the other side of Ashbourne. They brought him down to
Derbyshire on the twenty-sixth of March, the Sunday, and of
course he had his fourth birthday in April, two weeks later, so
he was only three when they brought him down from Leek that
Sunday, and he didn't remember anything about it, so he expected
he was asleep most of the journey. Of course the vicarage was
built in eighteen sixty-seven, and he had been living in Ockbrook
for quite a few years when they had the procession; that was in
eighteen ninety-seven, and he remembered the procession coming
up the road there as clearly as if it was yesterday, for the diamond
jubilee. They planted that lime tree by the war memorial, he saw it
planted himself, and they changed the name to Victoria Avenue.
And then the next autumn they planted the other trees up the
avenue. The bees loved that lime; he'd seen them swarm in it
dozens of times. Of course, he'd always been a farmer, but he
hadn't been farming properly for forty years, except for a few
ducks and that sort of thing, not since his accident. It was in
nineteen seventeen, right at the darkest time of the war, the
fourteen-eighteen of course, and they were loading a load of hay
on a cart, and he was up on top tying it down with rope to stop it
slattering; that was a Derbyshire word, slattering; yes, that was an
old Derbyshirism. And the rope broke, and all the other fellows
were buried in hay, but of course they didn't have far to fall
because they were standing down on the ground. But he came
down from the top, he fell from the top of the load, and when they
pulled all the hay off him there was blood coming out of his nose
and his mouth and his eyes and both his ears, and that old leg
was broken and his hip was out. And they took him to the in-
firmary and gave him up for dead, and for ten days they said there
wasn't a hope. But he got better, though mind you he had always
been a strong man; and he came out of hospital, but that was the
end of farming for him, in nineteen seventeen it was, right at the
darkest time of the war. He came to this house on March the first,
nineteen twenty-four; and the old vicar — that's the one before
this one, who was vicar for thirty-five years, of course he's passed
on now — the old vicar moved into the vicarage across the road
on the following Tuesday, March the sixth; and if there was a day
when they met and the vicar didn't pull his leg he knew there
was something wrong. Though he was a Methodist himself, of

course. Yes, he'd always been a strong man, but now he couldn't move without these sticks. Those fellows from the council or the ministry or something, surveyors he supposed you'd call them, they were for ever measuring the road and all that, up and down Victoria Avenue where they had the procession, trying to decide to build a bridge over the by-pass for the local people, or a tunnel underneath it. But he was always telling them they could never go underground here, they'd never do it, they'd run into water straight away. But they went on surveying all the same. And of course he didn't suppose they'd listen to an old country-man anyway.

The vicar took me up to a farm above Ockbrook, where suddenly we were in the Derbyshire countryside. He was bringing Holy Communion to the farmer's mother, a quiet, grateful, sorry old woman who sat by her parlour fireside where she had sat for half a century, with family wedding photos on the dark furniture and on the mantelpiece a tin of udder lotion. Her four sons were all farmers, but the eldest had turned fifty last week, and that made her feel old. While she made her communion I walked round the farm, through the mud and dung, with her son John, a rural district councillor with bent arthritic fingers and a rib cracked from a fall. He showed me his Friesian cows and his two bulls and the gleaming stainless steel dairy equipment, and said that the Conservatives had only just won at the last election and that with all the newcomers to Ockbrook it looked as though it would soon be lost to Labour; and he sounded as though he didn't mind.

On the way back we met an old warrior who had fought with Lawrence of Arabia, had flown a Bristol fighter during the march to Damascus and shot down a Turk in flames, and had later worked in Burma, Ceylon and Tanganyika. His son, who had a Malayan wife and lived high in the Peruvian Andes, had just come home to Ockbrook on leave and was trying to persuade the old man to go back with him to Peru. "Young people are not as adventurous as we used to be," he said, looking severely at me, "and if I was a young man now I'd go right away." But he felt old, and the thought of the altitude troubled him; besides, his wife was buried in Ockbrook, and he didn't like the idea of leaving.

As we drove on, the vicar told me a little about the curious feelings some of his parishioners held for the dead. One old widow, during a very cold spell, had confessed to him how glad she was her husband had been cremated; she would have hated to think of him lying out in the cemetery in that weather.

*   *   *

Ockbrook is a phenomenon of the age, a transitional place no longer rural but not yet fully urban. There is still the nucleus of the old red brick village and there are fields where at the end of February the first lambs were tottering, white and gawky. But there is more to it than that; there are the midlands of England smothering the cottages and farms with their great industrial mess; there are the Trent and the Derwent, sluggish with effluent and frothing with detergent; there are factories and mines, railways and canals, cableways and gasworks. The important things are the new things not the old — the housing estates advancing over the ploughed fields and the pylons striding over the hills, not the pigs grubbing among the cooling towers. The villagers are lost in the invasion.

"It's a suburb now," said the retired parish organist, who had come originally from the next village where he had been a choirboy. I called on him in his house on Sunday afternoon, and he came into the front room rubbing his eyes; he had had his dose at lunch-time, he said, which I think meant that he had been to the pub after morning service. He still felt a bit of a foreigner in Ockbrook, though he had lived in it for forty-five years; yet now the place seemed to belong to the people on the big council housing estate, most of whom hadn't even been born in Derbyshire; that estate, he said, was a wilderness.

He showed me a leather-bound book about his old village church that had been given to every member of the choir to commemorate the rebuilding of the organ in 1905; he kept it in a cardboard box, as a memento of the days when village choirs were properly trained, and he spoke of famous teachers who had come from West Hartlepool, Manchester and even Oxford to coach them. He himself had learnt to play the village organ and was studying for the Royal College of Organists when the Great War came and he joined the army and became a sergeant-major—bayonet drill and that sort of thing.

Even in the army he got some music. "There was a fellow called Langton, played the violin. He was a wizard. He could play anything. He played beautifully, really beautifully. You don't get playing like that nowadays. He could even be funny on his violin, he was so good. They sent him to France. I often wonder what happened to him. You would have heard of him, if you see what I mean. They all went to France, the musicians. But not the boxers; they were shielded."

After the war he came back and settled in Ockbrook, with a job at the factory that had been built while he was away to make aeroplane fabric and had now turned over to artificial silk. But his music had suffered: "You know what it's like. There was courting, and then marrying, and then having children. You can't just pick it up after a five-year break, not after all that bayonet drill. I could have been a pianist once; not the top, you know, but very good."

To show what he meant, he sat down at his piano and strummed great extravagant chords up and down the keyboard. Then imperceptibly he slipped into 'Jesu Joy of Man's Desiring', with lots of pedal and a strange fumbling technique with his fingers that made the house resound like a village organ when the organist has pulled out every stop. Then, as easily, it was some Chopin played the same way, and then, after more chords, a wayward fulsome piece that he must have found in the album on top of the piano, 'Harvest Moon Romances'.

On the walls were violent paintings, the work of the old organist's son, of fantasy aeroplanes fighting each other and church towers falling to ruin and misty lakes. The son had been in the air force during the second war and had flown a hundred and fifty missions over Europe, but whereas before the war he had been brought up as a good churchgoer and had sung in the choir with a fine tenor voice, he had come back a bolshie; not actually a Communist, but red enough. He had never married and had stopped going to church, but instead he had grown a beard and built a bungalow at the other end of Ockbrook where he now painted these pictures and filled his windows with stained glass. His father didn't understand him, or his other son, a railwayman who had also been brought up with church and all that, but now never went.

"The vicar's a lucky man, having a body of men like that in the choir. About eight men at evensong sometimes. You don't get that often in country parishes these days."

The vicar had other ideas: "Some people seem to think that the church exists for the choir." But he agreed about the big new council estate; it was a black spot, difficult to reach, where a car for every family and a new pram for every baby were the common aspirations, where occasionally through the big picture-windows one could see grubby trouserless kids playing round the television, and where the few patches of squalor were more the result of idleness and economic mismanagement than of need.

Ockbrook's hierarchy is a narrow affair. There is no squire and only a few doctors and small businessmen to supplement the clergymen in the middle class. Though it is becoming a dormitory for Derby factories, the senior managerial staff tend to live in one or two smart villages on the north side of the city, towards the pretty country, leaving Ockbrook to their underlings. When they heard I had never been in the county before, people would say to me, "You should really go up to the north; it's lovely up there," betraying a hint of inferiority and neglect; the Ockbrook football team holds the all-England record for never winning a match.

But if there are no millionaires, nobody is on the breadline either, and though Monday is still washing-day whatever the weather, there is no tradition of hardship as in some towns. A bright young businessman living in an old rectory on the smarter side of Derby said he thought it was because south Derbyshire had developed comparatively slowly and late, with an economy based on stable industries like agriculture and the railways, which had hardly suffered in the depression. Local politics reflect this mild climate. The chairman of the Ockbrook parish council, a lively Labour man only too well aware of the difficulties of settling the population of a big housing estate on a dwindling agricultural neighbourhood, said that the estate, with no church, no pub and no post office of its own, hardly thought of itself as a community at all. But to his sorrow the parliamentary seat was won at the 1959 election by a very unlively Conservative, with the smallest majority in England.

It is perhaps significant of the local view of politics that on a hoarding, between a Conservative poster boasting 'Straight talk and action' and a Labour poster proclaiming that 'People matter', was a third, keeping Home and Wilson at arm's length, announcing that 'All human life is there' every Sunday in the *News of the*

World. Human life in Ockbrook, at any rate, knows what's what when it comes to the important things.

Another advertisement was more poignant. The rich man in his castle a mile or two away was selling up, and the furniture was to be auctioned; already the estate had been bought by a gravel company, which would soon be tearing up the land with draglines and lorries, while the earl himself retired to the sanctuary of an Irish racing stables. The church by the castle, the very church where the old organist had once been a choirboy, was seldom unlocked; and the earl's great sullen park, his farms and villages — his farmers and villagers — waited gloomily for the profiteers.

*   *   *

The vicar took me one evening to the church hall, where he was leading the church men's fellowship team in a tiddlywinks match against the youth club management. He lost the game, but he won a bag of coal in a raffle, and afterwards a brave girl sat on the ping-pong table with a guitar and sang terrible folk songs, sometimes forgetting the words. It was better when she finished and the boys could turn on the gramophone again.

He took me up to the Settlement — the settlement of eighteenth-century buildings reached through a gate at the top of Ockbrook where there was the curious confidence of an ancient international community that spoke of its record of Christian perseverance through the centuries and across the world, and of Martin Luther as an upstart — the settlement of Moravians. We met the one-eyed Moravian minister tying up his roses outside the manse, and he took me to admire his burial ground, where the snowdrops and first blue crocuses were pushing up among the flat stone plaques lying on the grass graves. We had tea with the headmistress of the Moravian girls' school, where on a piano in the gym a pupil was spelling out Bach's first prelude, and in the science laboratory a Chinese girl from Hong Kong told me of her hopes of getting into Liverpool University; but in the entrance examination Liverpool, ever conscious of its sons, had made her write an essay on the significance of the cult of the Beatles, and poor little Chinese girl, she found it hard. The headmistress got down on her knees and spread across the floor great diagrams of Moravian history and photographs of schools in Holland and Switzerland and America but now only three of her staff and a dozen of her pupils were Moravians, though there were still more than a hundred in the Ockbrook settlement.

The vicar sent me up a hill in the other direction, with a school on top for sub-normal boys. "From the sons of company directors to the sons of coal-miners," said the headmaster, standing in front of the championship records of his wife's basset hounds. "Some of them never even learn to read." They had a pony and a donkey and goats and chickens, and an old bus standing on a concrete plinth in which teen-age youths played like little kids, going on make-believe journeys to the seaside and to home. If there wasn't much they could be taught, at least they could be made happy; and as I walked down the hill through the partridges, with the sun dropping like an egg-yolk among the power station chimneys, I wondered at the devotion of the man who had taught a demented fifteen-year-old boy to scrawl his own name and then sing for me, in a diabolical croak, 'I'm Popeye the Sailor Man'.

I met an old carpenter who was working in the house he was born in, making a new counter for the village post office. Not that it was a village any more, he said, what with the new housing estate. "We're the strangers here now; but these new people, they don't even know their own roads; they're always asking us the way." He demonstrated his machinery, still good after years of service, and showed me the old jack-planes he had inherited from his father and still used, re-mouthed with boxwood and re-soled with teak. Then his youngest daughter, a schoolgirl, came in with a pork pie to put in his bag and take up for his lunch at the post office.

I visited an old lady in a new bungalow on the estate, cheerfully absorbed with her bronchitis and her television. She couldn't go out any more, and her son at the other end of Ockbrook didn't often come and see her: "He thinks I'm all right." And so, in a way, she was. Once, when her husband was alive and working on the land of the old hunting earl, they and their five children had had to live on eighteen shillings a week; and after that almost anything in life was good. She could watch the sun coming in her window, and look out across her tiny garden to the traffic on the by-pass. "Some old people are so much worse off. They have crutches and can't feed themselves or dress or wash, but just sit in their chairs. Yes, I've a lot to be grateful for."

A neighbour, in another bungalow, with her hair almost fallen out and her garden overgrown and deep in leaves, was not so perky. Her son and daughter had died, and then her grand-daughter when still a girl; the old widow had a photo of her, but it was too unbearable to look at often, so she kept it in a drawer wrapped in a napkin, and on the mantelpiece was only a picture of herself before she married, looking beautiful in mutton-chop sleeves in front of a painted landscape. She drew the bungalow curtains to keep the light off her plastic tulips and her aspidistra, and to make the new room as much like the little old cottage she used to live in, now demolished to make way for the by-pass. Her only happiness, with all her family dead, was the regular visit of the vicar, the nicest they'd had in Ockbrook for a long, long time.

Then he took me to an old people's home. The red brick build-ings, with tiny tarmac yards and great boilers standing under a thick chimney, had once been the workhouse, and the grim old spirit had not been quite exorcised. We went into a room full of old women, sitting in almost silence and doing nothing at all; they were not knitting, nor reading, and hardly talking. It was as if, after that long life, there was nothing left to do but die. On a white table was a battered Sunday paper, a teacup and a bowl of artificial anemones. A crooked figure in a brown cardigan, one of the vicar's parishioners, said that she didn't seem to do anything these days; she didn't seem to knit, she didn't seem to watch the television, and though she had been in the home three years she didn't know where the library was; between six-thirty in the morning when she was woken up and nine at night when she went to bed, she was as inactive as a baby. Next week she was going home to Ockbrook for a fortnight, to stay with her son, and she asked the vicar about an old friend of hers there. "Oh, haven't you heard?" he said, and for an instant she looked terrified. He told her the news, and she said, "Goodness gracious, I thought you were going to say she's passed on." Death was her obsession. "Bless you," said the vicar as we left, and the terror on her face turned to gratitude.

We went into the women's ward where there was another parishioner, a deaf skeleton in a bed, motionless and waiting and not hearing the football match on the radio in the corner of the room. In the next bed was a woman with a goitre lying beside her on the pillow, like another eyeless head.

A nurse, a slim dark girl with a new wedding-ring on her finger, said, "Aren't you the vicar of Ockbrook?" She had come to him last year to have her banns read, and he remembered her and praised her for still working in the home: "Bless you," and I nearly cried.

Outside, across a yard, men were shuffling to their tea, madly, vaguely, sadly, gaily, in hope or in desperation or in pain or in a dream. One was hugging the wall, fondling each old corner of the brickwork and each familiar drainpipe; another, almost boyish with a lunatic eye and a long tooth sticking like a fag end from his lips, skipped round the yard and into the dining-room, his trousers flapping above his skinny ankles. Through a window I saw them lining up for their plate of bread and butter and their mug of tea, and suddenly I remembered that I had seen them all before—in an old film somewhere, or in photographs of that house in Singapore where they take the old Chinese to die, or in a picture by Hieronymus Bosch.

In the men's ward, in an atmosphere mixed from cheap tobacco, old breath, creased bodies and stained bedding, it was difficult not to wonder what the point of it was, and not to wander between the beds, as close as graves in a cemetery, and look at the empty heads as if they were strangers already dead; they didn't even stare. But then suddenly one toothless face twisted up and cried for the vicar, a high unearthly sob, weeping through the desolation; the man had been brought in only the day before, and there was nowhere in the world to go.

At the end, beyond the beds, a row of decayed figures sat in dirty dressing-gowns. At first, from a distance, they looked like ordinary living men, but on closer sight they dissolved. The man at the end of the row, who had seemed quite a toff with a grey moustache and a coloured handkerchief in the pocket of his check coat, disintegrated into a filthy being who took out his deaf aid, slowly unwound the flex and put it to his ear.

"Ninety last Monday," screamed the man in the next chair. "We had a cake for him. That's his picture on the wall." I looked, but the wall was empty. "On the wall there, his picture." I looked again, getting a little frightened, but there was nothing there.

Another man stood up and began to undo his pyjama trousers. A nurse shouted at him: "Not now. Can't you see we've got visitors? You only want to do it to annoy them." Sadly he sat down at the table, laid his head on a plate of bread and butter and went to sleep. Awake or asleep, it hardly made any difference.

We left, and walked down the corridor. Over a glass door – I couldn't believe it – was written 'Maternity Ward', and through it young mothers were suckling their babies.

XV

NEWMARKET

"FUNNY morning," said the barmaid. "Snow one minute, sunshine the next. But I think we've got a load to come." She went on about the weather, about March coming in like a lion, and about the terrible time they had had last year, with the gallops all frozen and no chance to exercise the horses. Then she leaned forward confidentially: "Brandy in a cup, I ask you! The things I get requested for. He's a proper charlie, he is. And you don't want to listen to a word he tells you about horses."

Horses are an obsession at Newmarket, and though they are no more the town's staple industry than fish at Lowestoft or coal at Blyth they are cherished much more jealously by the town's inhabitants. And not exclusively Newmarket horses, either. In the bar all eyes were on the clock, not because of closing time, but because somewhere in England that afternoon there was a race at two o'clock, another at two-thirty, and a third at three. Men sat sifting newspapers, comparing the promises of one tipster with another; men dashed out to the betting-shop; men—midget men with ageless faces, scarred or gaunt or bulbous or pitted, all looking as though you could slash the skin down to the veins and no blood would run out, but only a trickle of some unhealthy and faintly alcoholic, perhaps illicit, liquid—men, before saying anything else, said, "What won?"

Horses are the industry, the occupation, the universal object. Newmarket, on the borders of Cambridgeshire and Suffolk, belongs to neither county, but only to the Turf, to the paddocks and courses of the world. Its people know more about what's going on at Goodwood and Lambourn, even at the Curragh and Chantilly, than at Cambridge or Bury St Edmunds. They also know what went on last year on the Turf, and the year before, and every important year back to the time when Nell Gwynn lived down the road and King Charles sat in his summer-house on Newmarket Heath and watched the races. For Newmarket, 1939 was not the year war broke out, but the year Blue Peter won the Derby; and it matters less that Queen Boadicea lived in the next village than that Fred Archer was a Newmarket man.

There are the legends, a mixture of men and horses. There was Archer himself, the best jockey of them all, who shot himself "just up the road there", they say, as though it was a month or two ago, though it was before the turn of the century. There were horses dead long before anybody in Newmarket can now remember, but whose pedigree and record are holy writ. There was The Tetrarch, the terrible grey from Ireland, and Steve, the great Donoghue, who some say was greater even than Archer, and Hyperion, the little stallion that sired more winners than any other horse, and kings and rajas and gaekwars, and a Lord Derby for every generation. And there was the Earl of Orford who drove a carriage and four: four stags. One day out on the heath he met the foxhounds, and the pack picked up the scent of his stags and chased him five miles back to Newmarket; they were at his heels when the earl, swinging into the yard of the Rutland Arms, shouted to the ostler to shut the gates behind him as he rattled through; it was a close escape, "a photo-finish", said the man who told me.

"That little chap in the corner," whispered somebody in a pub. "He was the man who broke in Isinglass." It was better than to have been Prime Minister.

"You can't tell me anything about France, Argentine, Russia," said somebody else. "I know them all." He had been a stable lad in charge of consignments of bloodstock, but Newmarket is not a place for humility; there is too much tragedy around.

"Hyperion's jockey, he must have had thousands of pounds through his hands at one time, but now he's a poor man living at the other end of town."

"Now that yearling the colonel bought at the December sales; that's a useful horse."

"If you put an onion on the bar," said the barmaid, "they'll start laying bets on its weight."

"They do the football pools," said a man who didn't really belong there, "but they don't think much of it."

"Now I can tell you anything," said a little thin man with big boots and a big peaked cap, "anything you want to know about Newmarket. I've been with horses for forty years. I'm busy at the moment, but any time you like, ask me anything you like, and I can tell you. You'll always find me in here."

"You don't get the morning champagne parties like you used to."

"Did you ever see Thomond in the Gold Cup?"

". . . and Golden Miller never ran again. It killed him. I saw it."

". . . not for fifty years, not since Gainsborough won the Derby."

" . . . by Windsor Lad, he was."

"They're full of the past," said a man from a saddlery firm, "but what they're really interested in is this afternoon and what's going to win the three-thirty." He said it was an odd thing about Newmarket that although there was so much legend there was so little nostalgia; the Rutland Arms until recently had a famous bar full of furniture and prints which featured in countless stories and pictures, but when it was superseded by a modern bar no different to any other the customers never protested; they saw nothing wrong with the change; in fact they probably never noticed it, for nothing could distract them from their racing.

"Any luck today?"

"Do any good?"

There was Bob Rodrigo, who offered me snuff in the public bar of the White Hart and whose grandfather was picked up as a little boy by the English soldiers after the battle of Ciudad Rodrigo and named after it. And another Bob, a slobbering old Welshman with red eyes who had once been caught cheating at cards in the Conservative Club. His opponent protested, at which Bob grew angry and warned him off the race course, threatening to turn his gang on him if he dared show his face there. Bob had once been a thug to be frightened of, but now in his old age he lay in bed all day in a lodging-house until it was time to go drinking. Two months ago he collapsed in the bar and was carried out on a stretcher, and nobody ever expected to see him again; but Bob came back. And there was a third Bob, who had once been a brilliant young jockey, and who, like so many successful jockeys, found he was getting too heavy for racing. He took to drink to keep his weight down, and then he took to training. He trained for some major or other who went and died, and Bob lost everything. Then his house was pulled down by the council, and he had to have all his stomach taken out. It was a run of bad luck, after a promising beginning. Of course, a friend might occasionally give him a hundred quid or so, to help him along, but it wasn't the same. Bob was seen a week or two ago on a bicycle, riding out for somebody.

Tragedy is common in Newmarket, where the local industry happens also to be the sport of queens and business barons, and a poor man's drug; a poor man's downfall, too often. And ruling the industry from a stern building in the High Street, with a power more autocratic than any law court and with an authority to suspend and fine and warn off from which there is no appeal, is the Jockey Club.

At the end of the High Street a cinema was showing *Murder at the Gallop* with an air of permanency. And every morning strings of racehorses were walked through the streets and up on to the heath for exercise. With sunbeams splitting from the clouds the horses curved superbly over the skyline, suddenly breaking into a gallop and bounding up the hill behind a beech wood. Touts with binoculars sat in their cars by the roadside, studying the progress of each horse and adding their bit to the huge, beautiful scandal of it all.

The stable lads, slouched on blanketed horses, looked surly and half-witted, and in a racing-stables I watched tiny boys running in and out of orange doors loaded with hay, oats and manure. Some of them were still at school, some of them had been lured even from foreign countries in the hope of becoming jockeys, some of them were old men who had never ridden in a race, and some of them were girls.

"They're mostly bog Irish," said a formidable woman in check tweeds. "But we can't get the undernourished ones now. Everybody's too well fed these days. We used to get thin, clever boys from Dublin and the Gorbals, but now the thin ones are the ones who haven't got the brains to be a good jockey, and the bright ones haven't got the weight" — by which she meant they had too much.

There were two thousand horses in training at Newmarket, and each one cost its owner a thousand pounds a year. I asked a trainer what the secret was, and he said that bad horses never win a race, however well trained they are, and that any fool of a trainer can make a good horse win; the secret is to make mediocre horses win, by entering them for the right races and bringing them up to top form at the right moment.

The flat-racing season had not begun, but there was a point-to-point steeplechase on a windy hillside beyond the heath, where a thin crowd shivered in its sheepskins and watched two or three horses galloping round the countryside and out of sight behind the beer tent. Most people's thoughts were on another racecourse at the far end of England, and when a big open-air television set mounted on a scaffold was switched on for the Cheltenham Gold Cup the point-to-point was abandoned and even the bitter wind forgotten.

"Bad organisation," said a testy colonel afterwards. "And jolly poor racing, too. Not a patch on Cottenham last week. There we had a dead heat and a couple of photo-finishes. I won't come to this meeting again in a hurry."

The talk turned from horses to people, but the idioms hardly altered. "He was old Jack's nephew" or "His mother was a Richards" were tossed out in the same lordly way as they would say that a horse was by this stallion or out of that mare. "She married a bit of tinkle," said one old fellow with a wink, as if to say that she had a good chance in the Two Thousand Guineas.

But Newmarket Heath, the wide rolling Turf where it all began, was marvellous; and at night the March sky was so clear and starry that it might almost have been tropical, if it hadn't been so cold.

* * *

"That's a pub sign I painted," said Michael, as we drove through a village south of Newmarket, with Dawn Image, his brindle greyhound bitch, curled on the seat between us. Michael told me about her skill at coursing, and about the game-cocks he used to keep. Cumulus clouds rolled across the sky and the sun glowed on the ploughed fields where pheasants pecked happily, glad to have survived the shooting season.

There were no road signs to the coursing meeting, so as not to attract the anti-blood sports people, and we lost our way somewhere across the Essex border. In a lane we met a little Morris with a family of gipsies in the front and two greyhounds in the back; they were lost too. Then we met a military man in a van, also looking for the meeting; he was one of the stewards, so they couldn't start coursing without us. At last our little caravan, touring the countryside and asking for news at every farmhouse, came on a crowd of about thirty cars parked in a row across a lonely field; there was something almost felonious about them, or else it was that I myself felt a little guilty.

Out in the field in front of the cars a man in a red huntsman's coat sat on a big piebald horse—the judge. Beyond him another man, the slipper, crouched behind a bale of straw with two greyhounds on a double leash, one with a broad red collar and the other with a white. According to our programmes the greyhounds were called Expensive Garnet, a black bitch by Eton Gossip out of Girl Friend, and Linden Luke, a black dog by Linden Calypso out of Linden Hope; they looked too blasé to care about such splendid names. Around the cars was gathered a bunch of people hardly less grand, hardly less double-barrelled, than the greyhounds; and tied to their owners, or shut up in the cars, were another fifty greyhounds.

"Not so cold as at Cheltenham on Saturday," said a jovial baronet.

"What a Gold Cup!" said a strong grey-haired lady. That day three people told me in confidence that she was a daughter of King Edward VII.

"Not so many hares as there might be, today."

"Two Saturdays back they shot six hundred at Six Mile Bottom."

"Two years back they shot twelve hundred in a day."

"Do you run him on the track?" called a man from the window of a butcher's van, admiring the big fawn dog belonging to the gipsy family.

"We sent him down to Romford once, to train," said one of the gipsies, "but he got gastro-enteritis down there, so we pulled him back."

Suddenly someone shouted and we all looked across the field; all the dogs howled. A hare came galloping across behind the slipper's hide; when it passed in front of him, his two greyhounds leapt forward on their leash; he ran a few yards with them, and then slipped the leash and they bounded ahead. The hare streaked, but the greyhounds streaked faster.

It was a beautiful moment, when the dogs were slipped, and after thirty races during the day I still enjoyed it. They swung over the field, their spines rolling like the sea, in a straight, superb sprint to the hare.

But then, when they had almost caught it, the hare turned and the dogs, more clumsy, careered on before they could slow down to follow it. It dodged this way and that, half the size of the greyhounds and slower, but much more nimble. The judge on his horse cantered after the race, across the field and back again, almost into a wood and round behind the cars. The dog with a red collar caught the hare and snapped it dead; but the judge, giving the victory to the dog that had scored more points in the chase, pulled out a white handkerchief and waved it as he trotted back. We looked at our programmes.

"That's Linden Luke." A few minutes later another hare was galloping over the field, and two more greyhounds were slipped to chase it. And so it went on all day, while we ticked off the winners on our programmes, noting which dogs were to race against which in the next round, and making wise comments.

"That's a worker, a proper worker."

"In very rough trim, that dog, I'm afraid, very rough trim."

"The red's unsighted," as one greyhound went tearing off in the wrong direction.

"Old Miss What's-her-name, she knows a thing or two about breeding, don't you think? Just look at the way that dog's working. Very useful, I should say."

"They're just following the hare now; no wind left."

Sometimes the greyhounds sprinted straight up to the hare, killing it before it had time to turn, and it was all over in a few seconds; but usually the hare was chased far across the field and often it got away, leaving the dogs blowing and exhausted, though the hare had already been hunted over two or three fields by the beaters, whereas the dogs had been carefully cosseted. The shorter the run, the better the winner's chance in the next round, and after each race the greyhounds were rubbed down with oil and given a drink of tea, and sometimes a dash of brandy.

The beaters came over the hillside, thirty men dancing about on the ploughed skyline, yelling and waving white flags against the winter trees.

"Haven't got enough beaters, that's the trouble."

"Trouble is, they're beating against the wind."

Two elegant white greyhounds chased a hare under a gate and it got away, leaving them to trot back to the cars, puzzled and out of breath.

"No nose, these greyhounds," said an elderly man in a deep, slow voice, who looked vaguely out of place, a fellow non-member like myself. But unlike me, he could afford to be a little contemptuous: "Up in Norfolk we course salukis."

Another man capped him: "I once had a borzoi puppy that went straight into a gate going at about forty, and came out the other side unscratched."

"Down in Somerset we walk-up for hares. Much more fun than driving."

"Ever coursed at Petworth?" somebody asked me. "In front of the house there? Awfully jolly."

The steward came through the cars calling the names of the dogs for the next race: "Dawn Image! Latest Statement!"

"Here," said Michael.

"Here," said a woman's voice. The two owners led their dogs out to the slipper, who tied them to his leash. A pheasant scuttled across the stubble, the dogs barked and everybody laughed. Then almost immediately a hare appeared, the slipper ran forward to guide the two greyhounds, and then slipped them. Latest Statement, a puppy but already bigger and faster than Dawn Image, shot ahead and nearly caught the hare; it turned, and Dawn Image, turning quickly, found herself in the lead. Then Latest Statement caught up again, and the hare turned again, and Dawn Image was there again, anticipating the turn. And so it went on.

"Game little bitch of yours," said the baronet to Michael.

"Game as a pebble," said Michael, pleased that his dog was doing so well. I was pleased too, and when the judge came trotting back waving a red handkerchief for Dawn Image I felt proud to know her.

The coursing stopped for lunch, and the judge dismounted from his piebald horse to have his sandwiches, limping across to his car. I asked Michael if he had a wooden leg.

"No, he spilt soup on his knee and did nothing about it till it was too late. Had to have his knee-cap off."

We went off for beer and bread and cheese in a pub, where a man said, "Never seen such hares. Ooh, they're game! Running like stags."

In the afternoon the coursing moved to another field in search of more hares ("They shot six hundred at Six Mile Bottom," from the strong grey-haired lady), Dawn Image won her second round ("Game little bitch," from the baronet), and a bottle of whisky was raffled and won by one of the beaters ("Good show, good show," from us all). Then we moved to a third field, and suddenly I saw the cubes and triangles of Harlow New Town shining in the distance from another world.

The last race of the afternoon ended with most people sitting in their cars sheltering from the wind. The hare slipped away from the two greyhounds and dodged through the line of cars to freedom.

"Did you see that?" cried one of the gipsies. "It was winking as it went past."

"And not a muscle moved on the face of the decayed Roman emperor," said a deep, slow voice behind me. I turned and saw the elderly saluki man from Norfolk. He pointed through the window of an old American car where an extraordinary face was sitting inside the turned-up collar of a teddy bear coat, and said, "This game attracts the oddest people." Then he looked at me again, and added, "Really the oddest."

*   *   *

In the countryside around Newmarket, among the pheasant woods and across the rich East Anglian fields where peewits forage in the plough, are the studs — gabled mansions with sham Tudor windows, white-painted clock-towers with equestrian weathercocks glinting through the beeches, immaculate thatched stables spreading to the ranch-like fences, paddocks sheltered by tall trees with sleek horses grazing — worlds away from the touts and bookies and hubbub of the racecourse. There is an air of peace and riches, and perhaps slightly of New England.

The most important inhabitants of the studs — the hosts who provide the money for the mowing-machines and white paint and the owners' pockets — are the stallions. Each stud has one or two of them, living in luxurious stables and occasionally being put out into special paddocks surrounded by high fences to stop them getting too excited when a mare walks past. And every year each stallion covers, as they say, forty mares.

A great stallion like Hyperion, whose sons and daughters and grandchildren so splendidly justified his colossal covering fee, can bring in a hundred thousand pounds a year from the owners

6*

of the forty mares he covers, and go on doing it for twenty years; so it is understandable that a life-size bronze statue of Hyperion now stands by the roadside outside the stud where he lived so long and covered so profitably.

But if a successful stallion's life is the voluptuous dream it appears, that of a successful mare is just one long pregnancy. Gestation for a horse lasts eleven months, which means that she has got to be covered again pretty soon after foaling. The covering season runs from the middle of February to the end of June, and the mares arrive at the stud in time to have their foals and be covered at their first cycle nine days later, and again at every three-week cycle during the season until the vet pronounces them pregnant. Sometimes the end of June comes and a mare has not conceived; but the stallion has done all he can, the mare is sent home in disgrace, and her owner has to pay the full fee.

Life in a stud is something between a harem and a maternity clinic. Men in long white jackets sit up all night, looking through little windows to the stalls where the mares are foaling; buckets of antiseptic stand around, and special oats are measured out, as if for patients on a diet, from galvanised bins; charts hang on the walls, and it would not be surprising to learn that flowers are sent to the mares after their confinement; instead, they are put out into paddocks with their foals, to convalesce and recover strength for their next pregnancy. At the stud I went to, a 'teaser' an Arab stallion with not too lustful a temperament, was ridden down the paddocks every afternoon to see how the mares were getting on; and any mare thrilled enough to whinny at him was marked out for covering next day.

I was told to be at the covering shed at ten-thirty in the morning, and just as the clock-tower chimed the stallion was led from his stable across the yard and in through the big double doors; at the same moment the mare, separated from her nine-day-old foal for the first time, was led in through the opposite door. The two horses were introduced.

It was a splendid big shed, fit for the purpose, with bales of straw piled six feet high round the walls and a deep mattress of straw spread across the floor. Execution was to be done, and as the doors were shut and the horses led to confront each other there was a feeling far more momentous than just another tick on a chart in the stud office. The stud groom and his three assistants hardly said a word, but it wasn't the silence of routine so much as of excitement and wonder.

The horses met across a high gate padded with coconut matting. For a moment they nuzzled each other over the top, and the mare kicked the gate. Then suddenly the stallion reared up on his hind legs and snorted; he tossed his black mane and curled back his upper lip with ferocious salacity; he had won the St Leger a few years ago, and he wasn't going to wait.

The gate was folded back to the wall and the mare was led by two of the grooms into the middle of the shed. Thick felt padded shoes were strapped to her rear hooves, in case she struggled, and the stud groom sponged her parts with antiseptic and bound up her tail with a bandage. The stallion, held by one groom, stood looking at her from behind, frisking and tossing his head. Perhaps, after all, he was going to take his time.

"Come on, come on," said the groom, coaxing quietly, and the stallion stamped the straw and snorted. Nobody else said anything, and the mare stood patiently, generously, waiting. "Come on, come on." The stallion walked away, leading the groom round the shed, and then reared up and punched the air with his forelegs. "Come on, come on," and the groom led the stallion back to the mare. Slowly his organ descended, swinging down towards the straw; but still he wasn't going to be hurried, and still he stood tossing his head and pawing. He reared again, his tail and forelegs lashing, his teeth bared. Then he made up his mind, and walked straight up to the mare, lifted himself gloriously up and lay across her back, snorted through his nostrils and nibbled her ears. The stud groom snatched the mare's tail aside, and suddenly she groaned, a faint high-pitched sigh from deep inside. For a moment the horses heaved, churning on the straw across the shed; then, as suddenly, they parted.

"Not covered," said the stud groom gently.

"Come on, come on," and the stallion stood looking at the mare again, tossing and rearing. Then he advanced once more and mounted her, but again he failed.

"Come on, come on." The quiet, kind voice of the stallion's groom and the silent respect of the others, the patience of the mare and the nobility of the stallion, transformed the covering shed into a theatre for a magnificent performance. The men might so easily have been bawdy, but instead they were polite, and it was beautiful.

The stallion came on a third time, hissing and arched and terrific. He mounted the mare swiftly and in a moment, with a scream from one of them, they were locked. They staggered across the covering shed in great heaves, uttering awful unearthly noises, and then they were still, while the heritage of a St Leger winner drained away.

"Covered," said the stud groom quietly; he too was satisfied, and moved by the experience. The stallion withdrew, and the horses stood apart on the straw, at peace. Then the mare was led out into the sunshine, back to her foal, and the stallion back to his stable across the yard. It had lasted just a quarter of an hour and had cost somebody three thousand pounds, and at three-thirty that afternoon the stallion would be doing it again with another mare.

"Well," said the stud groom to me, "perhaps you've seen a Derby winner got." I thanked him for letting me watch, and felt a little guilty that I had enjoyed it so much.

XVI

CERNE ABBAS

THERE was none of the sense of spring that there had been at Newmarket the day before. In the country bus from Sherborne, besides myself and a fat schoolgirl with a satchel and a double chin and the surly driver who grumbled whenever he had to get up and open the door for a passenger, there were eight women on their way home from shopping; from their hoots and shrieks they might have been drunk. But outside the rattling windows fine, cold rain was driving over the hills, as though the winter still had a long way to go in Dorset.

The driver put me out by a row of cottages, and the bus disappeared. I took a side road, curling up a hill among fat beech trees, and walked for half an hour along a lonely ridge above the darkening valleys. It was weird, impalpable country, and the feeling was enhanced by my having no idea what to expect at the friary. I dropped down a steep lane between high hedges, and came to a crucifix standing in the corner of a field. Then I came to a shilling lying on the ground, and then a penny. Perhaps they had been jettisoned by some guilty Franciscan, ashamed of his riches. I picked them up and put them in my pocket—my thirteen pence.

At the bottom of the hill lay the friary, like a collection of domesticated farm buildings, with a big kitchen garden beyond and a car park across the road. I met an elderly man in corduroy trousers who led me into a house, put me in a little room in front of a boiler and told me to get dry. He left me, and as I warmed my hands I remembered having seen a bundle of white cords hanging over the banisters of a staircase, and an Annunciation on the wall; but my preconceptions of what the friary was going to be like were already fading, and by the time the door opened and a young man with wide, kind eyes and bristly hair, wearing a friar's brown habit and sandals, came in and held out his hand, I had already forgotten.

"Good afternoon. I'm Brother Angelo."

From the first I began to wonder what Brother Angelo had been before he became a friar. From his confident, urbane manner, his distinct voice and his ability to switch at a moment from piety to hilarity, he might have been an actor; from his elegant gestures and the sight of him once gently wiggling his hips inside his habit and clicking his fingers, he might have been a dancer; from his wit and gaiety he would have been the life and soul of any party he was at. But then I learnt that he had been a ladies' hairdresser in Chelsea, sharing a basement flat off the King's Road. Now his experience came in useful as the friars' barber, and although he was still only a novice he had already made a reputation for himself as a travelling preacher; and from his love of his new life and his utter dedication to the Society of Saint Francis he could only have been a friar.

He told me that the building we were in, the friars' house, was silent, except on Saturday afternoons between sext and compline; and he took me out and beyond the hedge surrounding it, where we could talk. He showed me the three chapels of the friary, and the three libraries, Saint Clare's parlour, the television room, the basket-weaving room, the tailor's shop, the games room, the burial ground, and the refectory. In the Juniper Library was a grey old man in a grey old suit playing chess with a young man in sideboards and winkle-pickers, and two boys reading by a log fire; and Brother Angelo told me about the home provided by the friars for men stranded on the fringe of society, and for boys who had been rescued from delinquency or who suffered from some physical or mental disorder that prevented them leading a normal life in the world. Twelve miles away was a school run by the friars for maladjusted boys; and in the east end of London, in Cambridge, in Northumberland, in Central Africa and in New Guinea were other houses of the Society, where friars taught and preached and followed the three-fold Franciscan vows of poverty, chastity and obedience.

Suddenly, in the courtyard outside Saint Francis' chapel, a bell rang, and Brother Angelo broke off in mid-sentence and stood in silence. It rang three times, and then another three, and a third three, and then it rang nine times. When it stopped Brother Angelo crossed himself: "That's the Angelus. Ten past six. All the friars freeze on the spot when it goes. But you don't have to."

He took me back to the friars' house and upstairs to my cell, a little white room with a bed, a chair and a crucifix, and a hot water pipe running under the window. Over the door was written 'Saint Leonard of Porto Mauricio', and through the thin partition wall came a smell of tobacco from the friar next door.

"Brother Patrick," whispered Brother Angelo. "He has a very bad spine and can hardly sleep for the pain, so don't disturb him." He left me to go to evensong, and warned me that supper, like breakfast, was a silent meal.

In the refectory I was put next to Father Oswald, the father guardian of the friary, who said a prayer and grace, and we all sat down in silence. Immediately there was a great passing of plates and mugs, a great dashing to and from the kitchen hatch by the friars whose turn it was to serve, an ostentatious pointing to the bread or salt, a hopeful catching of eyes and prodding of elbows, a mute miming of a great silent 'Cocoa?' At the same time a grey-headed friar standing up at a lectern underneath a picture of the Last Supper — a man who had once been an officer in the Indian army — began to read aloud from a theological criticism of Eliot's poetry.

It was nice not to have to make conversation to strangers or spend time explaining myself, when there was so much I wanted to watch. Brother Patrick, in a skull cap and a little black beard, came in with a stick and sat down before grace was said; he swallowed a pill and was given a special plate of tinned salmon. The rest of us had bowls of thick onion soup and mugs of cocoa, and at intervals down the tables were big discs of cheddar cheese. There were about thirty friars in the room, with another thirty men and boys belonging to the home sitting among them. At one of the tables a joke was going on, with silent laughs. I saw Father Oswald making signs to me, and wondered how long he had been doing it and what he meant; finally he gave up and whispered "More!" in my ear, holding a ladle of onion soup over my plate.

The friar at the lectern finished the passage about Eliot and changed to a biography of Martin Luther King, while we changed to dried dates and more cheese. Brother Angelo, opposite me, looked scandalised at hearing of a black woman in an Alabama bus being turned out of a seat reserved for whites; and at the climax of the story, when we had all finished eating, the reading went on in a silent room. Somewhere a friar burped. When the reading stopped Father Oswald said grace, and we all went out into the night.

I went into the Juniper Library and was tackled by the young man in sideboards who had been playing chess. This was a beautiful place, he said, with a beautiful family living in it; it ought to be the temple of the new Jerusalem; it must have been what Blake had in mind. Even my own arrival at the friary, he knew, was not my own choice: "Our father has his reasons for everything." It wasn't just a coincidence that he and I should meet here. One day soon he was going to set out with twelve chosen companions for a beautiful valley in the mountains of South America, which he had once visited as a child; there they were to found a settlement where all their needs would be supplied by providence, where worries and wars and money and politics and work would exist no more, where they would start a race of human beings that would bring peace and perfection and beauty to the world for ever. There was no other name for the settlement but paradise, and although lots of the details had still to be worked out, he wasn't worried; everything would simply just happen, according to a plan, like my arrival; as soon as he saw me he knew that I was to be one of his chosen twelve.

A touch of dementia, I supposed; and another boy in the Juniper Library, who restlessly plied me with questions — "You're a Sussex man, aren't you? Where do you live in Sussex? Do you know you have a Sussex profile? How can I write? What would I write about? How could I get paper to write on? Would anyone read what I wrote?" — was just another kind of madman. Feeling slightly deranged myself, I fled to Saint Francis' chapel. On the way I met Brother Aquinas who said, "I expect you tumbled pretty quickly to those two, didn't you?" He told me that they had several people in the home who had been psychiatric patients and who came for a month or a year or even for life; as with the ex-borstal boys and the ragged old misfits, the friars didn't pretend to give them professional treatment, but only peace and a home, where they might become aware of belonging to a family grown round a community living according to a strict and constant rule, infused with happiness and inspired by a supernatural power.

There was plenty of peace in Saint Francis' chapel that night. It had once been a cow-shed, and its long white-washed walls

straddled by black beams still kept something of the farm. Fourteen little red crosses were fixed in a row along one wall — the
Stations of the Cross — and the crucifix on the altar was draped in
purple for Lent. There was no other colour, except the brown
habits of the friars facing each other across the narrow stone
floor.

That night, before compline, there was an hour of silence; the
candles scarcely flickered, and the whiff of incense was a suggestion more than a fact. A friar yawned, another clicked a rosary,
and holiness filled the chapel, lapping round the little wooden
chairs and wrapping over us like a great warm comfort.

At nine o'clock an acolyte tinkled a bell, and the friars' seventh
service of the day began. The simple plainsong chanted by two
dozen men was as moving as the silence had been, and then one
of the friars walked over to an old upright piano and they sang a
vigorous hymn. Father Oswald led prayers for the friars of the
Society in other parts of the world, invoking the help of Saint
Francis and Saint Clare; and at the end they lifted their brown
pointed hoods over their heads, bowed to the altar and filed out
to their cells.

*   *   *

"May Jesus Christ be praised," said Brother Angelo, opening
my door at dawn.

"Amen," I snored back at him, trying to control my temper
with the thought that he had been up at five-thirty for matins.

We had porridge and prunes for breakfast, with readings from
a biography of Pope Pius XII, and afterwards the friars went back
into chapel for terce and their chapter of faults before changing
into working clothes. Brother Desmond, a black friar from the
West Indies, allotted me work in the garden.

All morning I carried glass cloches for lettuces from one end of
the garden to the other, with a young man who had recently
served three months in prison for attacking his wife's lover, and
with Brother Dominic, the youngest novice in the Society, who
had been a shop-window designer before becoming a friar four
days after his twenty-first birthday, against his parents' will; since
he was a boy he had come to feel that a religious life was going to
be inevitable, and when he first stepped into Saint Francis' chapel
he knew that he was to be a Franciscan.

"First morning of spring," said an old man in a dirty jacket and patched tweed trousers. "I've put it in my diary."

"There were lepers in Saint Francis' day," said a friar in khaki shorts, "but we can't get them now, so we have these old men instead."

"This is the first morning for thirty years that I haven't had a beer," said a man I couldn't place, wearing an Eton tie. Then he said he had been a stockbroker, and would give anything to see the racing at Sandown Park that afternoon.

Sometimes, that first morning, I found it hard to tell who was a friar in working clothes and who was one of the motley people they had rescued from some tragic limbo. There was a young American college boy who had been lost on a round-the-world scooter trip and was waiting for his parents to send him the money to get home. There was a bishop in a purple cassock, on a retreat. There was a poor fellow with a stammer so bad that all morning he never finished a sentence. There was a weird, gentle character in check plus-fours and a Norfolk jacket who continuously pushed an empty wheelbarrow. There was Brother Angelo in tight jeans and a sweater, and Brother Selwyn who had been a telephone operator in New Zealand, and Father Donald who had been a sailor, and Brother Alan who had been training for the Methodist ministry, and Brother Jeremy who had taught English at a minor public school, and Father Chad who had been a parish priest on Tyneside, and Father Silyn who had once confessed at the morning chapter of faults that "Yesterday I swore at the chickens, in Welsh", and a friar who had been a successful engineer with a big house and two cars, and another who had owned his own business and had a daughter and at one time a wife who had been killed in an air crash. There was a twisted old man who appeared from behind a pile of logs each time I walked past and said, "Hello, Nicholas." There were chickens running in a pen, and there was a donkey which brayed, adding a nice Assisi touch and offsetting the bishop's Rover in the car park.

Walking past the novices' house carrying two cloches, I saw Brother Derek up a ladder, painting a window. Suddenly he slipped and knocked his paint pot off, and it spilt white paint across the grass below. An oath rang out across the friary, just as Brother Cuthbert — or Brother Bede, I never learnt the difference — walked past: "Ha, Brother Derek! That will be for the chapter of faults tomorrow. I know you won't forget. In fact, I think I'll remind you myself."

Half way through the morning we broke off for cocoa in the court outside Saint Francis' chapel, and I asked a friar why they didn't keep cows and pigs and try to make a success out of farming. A friar's life, he said, was not at home on a farm, but out in the world, in the Society's missions, in parish pulpits and schools and prisons; some friars might find their best work was connected with the home, just as others had a flair for evangelical or social work, but any of them could be sent by the Society to another field, and apart from the novices very few of the friars remained permanently at the friary.

Lunch in the refectory was a noisy meal, and I was surprised, almost shocked, at the friars' boisterousness, which sometimes touched irreverence, until I remembered also their astonishing reverence. With chapel and work filling a sixteen-hour day, there was little time left for talking; and lunch, for forty minutes between sext and none, was one of the few chances for the friars to indulge their high spirits.

"Some of us may be homosexual," said the friar next to me, "or heterosexual, or bi-sexual. But we simply haven't got time for any of them. We all feel like going out on the razzle sometimes, and so it's a good thing that our life is as full as it is. We have no time to stop, no time to lie back and daydream, no time to think or to wish. Certainly we love; love is the only thing a good friar needs. We love God and the church and Saint Francis. We love these nasty old men and these half-witted boys. We love each other, which perhaps is why we touch each other so much; you may have thought it a bit queer when you first saw a friar clasping another one."

"Sometimes we hate each other, too," said a friar across the table. "After all, what would you expect, with such an odd bunch of human beings? We're always running along to the father guardian and telling tales about each other."

"Too often," said the first, "one feels, what the hell! Why should I wear these silly clothes? Why should I do what the father guardian says? Why should I get up at half past five in the morning when all these old men and boys we look after are still asleep? Why should I go to chapel again when I've been five times today already? People say it must be so easy, with everything provided for us by a lot of rich old ladies; and they think the habit is just too glamorous for words. But it's darned hard, and there are times when we just want to sit back and watch the television."

"If Perry Mason hasn't solved his murder by compline tonight there'll be trouble," I heard a friar say, further down the table.

"Obedience," said Brother Columba, in the kitchen next morning. "Obedience is far the hardest vow to keep. Once you have accepted obedience, poverty and chastity are simple." He was in charge of the kitchen, and set me to peel onions and slice them. When he saw my eyes running he began to sing a hymn: "Drop, drop, slow tears; and bathe those beauteous feet." It was his onion hymn, and he had another one for every vegetable. His passion was Sweden, where he had been several times, working among young people in a ski resort. He said there was nothing like a sauna bath for getting people to talk; when they had no clothes on, they dropped their other inhibitions too. And his dread was to be sent to New Guinea; whenever the father guardian brought the subject up, Brother Columba would say, "Now father, please don't let's talk about that again. You know I like my young men to be civilised." He had a great laugh and a rich Irish voice and a shaven head, and his kitchen was full of wit and merriment.

"Saint Francis might raise an eyebrow here and there," said Father Chad. "It's not just that we wash more often than he did, but it's a bit trickier trying to live in poverty in England in the twentieth century than it was in Italy in the thirteenth." The friars have no money, and cannot be given it or inherit it. When they travel they are given a railway ticket, but they are expected to hitch-hike as much as possible, and they have friends all over the country who they know will give them food and shelter. Their brown habits are made in the friary tailor's shop, and only their sandals and underclothes have to be bought. ("It's a bit galling to have to go to the father guardian and ask for a new vest.") But it is a different matter for the Society, which has to have funds for its work; and the difficulties of reconciling viability with poverty raise constant problems: Is the food too good and plentiful, or would the friars be unable to work so hard on less? Are newspapers and a television set justified on the grounds that it is impossible to know about the modern world without them? Is central heating a breach of austerity when there are so many old men and boys living in the friary? How can the friary exist in the middle of the Dorset countryside without a car? A balance is reached by letting the Society have money to continue its work, while the friars individually follow a true Franciscan life.

The father guardian told me that the Society's changing emphasis from preaching to prison and borstal work was having an effect on the friars. Very few of the new novices had a university degree, but in a non-academic community that was no disadvantage; there were no great scholars among the friars, because there would be nothing for them to do, and some of the other religious houses of the Anglican church, where the atmosphere tended to be more like a dons' common room, had reason to envy the Society of Saint Francis for the number and youthfulness of its novices. And just as the friary buildings were no more monastic than any other Dorset farm, so it was with the friars. "We are a brotherhood of individuals," he said, "voluntarily united by our vows. We don't try to stamp out the novices in a mould."

About half the novices never finish their three-year novitiate. They can be released from their vows at a moment's notice, if either they or the Society feel that it is a mistake to continue. Sometimes it is the rigour of the life that defeats them, or the psychological strain, or the long, enclosed months that they have to spend in the more monastic atmosphere of another house of the Society; but usually it is a feeling that they can serve humanity more usefully in another way, and those that leave the Society are never considered to have failed. A few even of those who go on to make their first three-year profession leave before it is finished. But once they have made their life profession, which by the rules of the Society cannot be done before the age of thirty, there is no turning back.

*   *   *

On my last afternoon I walked up into the mist and across the hills to see the great man of Cerne Abbas. There he was, swinging over the Dorset downs above the old village, wielding his club and showing off his huge manhood. I ate buttered toast in a tea-shop, and the proprietor, waiting in boredom for Easter and the first coach-load of the season, told me maliciously that the village girls still go up and sit on the giant, as their ancestors had done to cure their infertility, but nowadays just for the thrill.

I walked back to the friary, and in Saint Clare's parlour I found Brother Colin, reading a paperback and chain-smoking cigarettes. For four months he had been a postulant, but at dawn next day he was going to take his novice's vows and exchange the black postulant's cassock for a brown Franciscan habit. The money he had brought with him from the world outside was almost finished, and he was spending the last few shillings frantically on cigarettes.

As with most friars, the call had come to Brother Colin not as a sudden voice from heaven but as an imperceptible awareness, growing over the years from a suspicion to a certainty. There was nothing very intellectual or introspective about him, but he was driven by a simple love of humanity; and nothing was more human about him than his nervousness the day before becoming a friar.

He was now twenty-five, and it had all begun in a railway restaurant car seven years earlier, when Colin — or rather Michael, as he was then — was a waiter. Two friars had come down the train and sat down at a table for lunch. "Crikey!" said the head steward. "Monks!" And because none of the other waiters had felt inclined, Colin found himself serving them.

There had then followed a chapter of coincidences when, over the years, one or other of the friars turned up again in his life: "It was pointed, wasn't it? I just had to come here." But it was not a matter of submitting passively to fate so much as becoming slowly conscious that sooner or later there would be nothing left to stop him taking the final, joyful step. There had been plenty of difficulties: he had been teased about the problems of chastity, and he had been tormented, after the experience of his first silent day as a postulant, by the prospect of nine months' contemplation in an enclosed house during his novitiate. There had also been compensations: though there was already a Michael in the Society, he had been able to use his own second name, and was spared from suffering with some exotic early Christian saint under a name he didn't feel he could carry off; and within a few hours of taking his vows he had an appointment in a prison, where he could begin to demonstrate a little of the compassion that had turned him from a frivolous young man in the tunic of a British Railways waiter into a wiser one in the brown habit and white cord of Saint Francis.

"May Jesus Christ be praised." Brother Angelo woke me next morning at twenty to six, on his way to matins. Half an hour later I slipped in at the back of Saint Francis' chapel, in time for the clothing of Brother Colin. Folded up on a table in the middle of the chapel lay a new brown habit, with a white cord coiled on top and a candle and a book and a jug beside it. A vase of daffodils stood on a whitewashed window sill of the old cow-shed; it was the first time I had seen flowers in that austere place, and they must have been put there to soften the awful ceremony that was to take place.

At the end of matins and before Holy Communion — at the end of a sleepless night of chain-smoking and before the sun was up — Brother Colin was clothed. Still in his postulant's black cassock, he knelt in front of the purple and gold robes of the father minister, between the two rows of friars.

"My son, what is thy desire?"

"I desire the mercy of God, and the religious life and habit."

"Dost thou believe that thou art called by God, and not moved by self-will or fancy?"

"I do so believe."

"Dost thou promise to remain in the holy state of chastity?"

"I promise so to do."

Then Brother Colin, having taken the oath of obedience to the Society of Saint Francis, stood up and faced the other friars: "Brethren, pray for me."

The father minister, sprinkling the new habit with water from the jug, prayed to Jesus Christ, "who didst deign to put on the clothing of our mortality", to bless and hallow the habit, "the token of purity and lowliness, that this thy servant, who through loving devotion desireth to put on the garb of holy religion, may be inwardly clothed with the garment of righteousness." He handed the habit to Brother Colin, saying, "The Lord put off from thee the old man and his deeds, and be thou renewed in the spirit of thy mind."

Brother Colin was led out to the vestry, carrying the folded habit, while we sang a psalm; and a few minutes later he was led back, clothed as a friar, the habit still creased with its newness.

"The Lord put on thee the new man, which after God is created in righteousness and true holiness."

Then the father minister called on God, "who to redeem the bondservant didst will that thy Son should be bound by the hands of ungodly men", to bless the white Franciscan girdle, and he tied it round Brother Colin's waist: "The Lord turn thy heaviness into joy and gird thee with gladness." He presented to the new friar the lighted candle, "the light of Christ, the token of thy immortality", and then the book, the Rule of the Society of Saint Francis. And he ended with Saint Francis' blessing: "The Lord bless you and keep you; the Lord make his face to shine upon you and be gracious unto you; the Lord lift up his countenance upon you and give you peace; the Lord bless you."

Brother Colin, once a railway restaurant car waiter called Michael, was now a penniless friar, with the terrible vows behind him and only half a packet of cigarettes to his name. We stumbled out into the morning; and because it was the day of the clothing of a novice, we had boiled eggs for breakfast, and no silence.

XVII

BURNLEY

I WANTED a normal English town, an antidote to the eccentricities of horse-racing and evangelising, where I might find people simply practising the ordinariness of being English. I decided on a Lancashire cotton town, partly because I had never been to one, and partly because I suspected that no such thing exists any more, and that in the place of the traditional soot-blackened, clog-clattering mill town I would find something more typical of the brash new Lancashire that, in its turn, is a symptom of modern England. Like Leek and Bridgwater and Wisbech it would be unique; but like them it would be slowly heaving itself from one incarnation to another, never quite sloughing off the old and never quite achieving the new. I chose Burnley.

It was late at night on the Friday before Easter week, more than seven months after the Butlin's holiday camp; I had changed trains at Manchester and again at Accrington, and now I was in a little diesel hooting over the viaduct between Burnley Barracks and Burnley Central. That viaduct spans old Burnley, and the three-minute journey between the two stations is a comprehensive tour; over the brick parapet you look down into hell, down through the fallen roofs of empty mills, into ten thousand tiny chimney pots, into the eyes of a people tossed by booms and slumps as lightly as the fluff that grows round the seed of a cotton-plant. Nothing had changed, except by depression and decay.

Twenty minutes later Burnley had swung the other way. It wasn't Lancashire, it was hardly England, it was more like Denver. I had expected bed and breakfast in the usual ghastly hotel but instead I found a skyscraper, only slightly stunted and not yet begrimed, in the middle of the town. I walked across the hall to the reception desk, straightening my tie and not hiding my surprise.

"So you didn't know we all wore clogs in Lancashire?" said a tantalising girl, giving me a shiny pamphlet and flapping a huge pair of purple eyelids. Then she dropped her voice about an octave and said, "But nowadays we take them off in bed."

"I've never been to Burnley before," I said to the porter who took me up in the lift, "and I never expected this sort of thing."

"Lucky man, never to have been here," he said. "I've spent all my life trying to get out."

I looked at the shiny pamphlet. It said welcome, in English and French. Welcome to meals and drinks served in my room if I wanted them. Welcome to a valet and a chambermaid and a taxi. Welcome to a radio and television and a morning newspaper. Welcome to a confidential secretary and a dictaphone. Welcome to a charge of three guineas a night, and another eight and six for breakfast, and ten per cent for tips — "there is no need for further payment." (I wondered if I was welcome to the girl at the reception desk; and I remembered that Butlin's had given me a big shiny welcome, too.) Welcome to Burnley, one of the most progressive towns in the north of England, to its museum and library and parks and open spaces, and to some of the most beautiful country in England, only ten minutes from the town centre. Welcome to the eighty-one thousand people of Burnley, characteristically rising to the challenge of the decline of the cotton trade, for "the native wit and skill of the loom operative is said to enable him to adapt easily — *ouvrier ou ouvrière, car il existe une tradition de travail parmi les femmes du Lancashire.*" What would Gracie Fields say to that, I wondered?

I went into the bar — a kind of bamboo airport style imposed on good old solid Lancashire, where there was a Chinese waiter in a blue tuxedo much too big for him — and ordered a double whisky and a ham sandwich; they cost the earth, so I had another double whisky. There were two dizzy red-headed girls together on bar stools, with refined Lancashire accents ("Walter asked me to go to Portugal with him, but I told him to stuff it"), and a silly English businessman trying to meet a bright young Frenchman half way ("*Ah oui, mais . . .* no British government would ever swallow that *. . . n'est-ce pas? . . .* I mean to say"), and a colourless, almost translucent man who might have been from Frankfurt or Zürich or Warsaw ("You know what my daughter says about the Beatles?"), and an American in the corner ("After twenty-four hours in Rome I didn't want to see the Pope anyway"). Two

English company representatives, far from home and trying not to look like commercial travellers, introduced each other to their girl friends: "Maureen here says she's Irish, but you don't want to hold it against her." "Brenda was the best thing that came out of that conference in Manchester last year." The girls were unbelievably artificial, so that it was a surprise to find they could make a human noise.

Half-heartedly I tried to make conversation with the two redheads perched at the bar, but they were the same kind; besides, they knew what they were worth. One looked all the way down to my feet and said, "Of course, there's stacks of brass up here." The other swivelled away from me on her stool and said, "I think it's a working town, really." So I bought myself a third double whisky.

I had been aware of the murmur of voices and bursts of clapping coming from some unseen festivity, and suddenly a waiter walked over to a corrugated wall beyond the bar and rolled it back. Into the room stepped a little old woman in a mauve evening dress, with the mayor, his gold chain hanging across the shoulders of his dinner jacket. Behind them followed four more women in long dresses, and a bishop in a purple frock coat, and then more women, and a few men, and many, many more women. They poured in, thick on to the floor round the bar, and the air was filled with squeals and chatter. It was a riot of gold lamé bursting under tension, of pink satin and violet muslin, of middle-aged spreads shimmering with sequins, of double chins straining at cultured pearls and bosoms heaving out of cultured furs, of dimpled elbows and peroxide curls and bulging feet, of lifted faces and dropped wombs, of women whose *embonpoint* might have made them magnificent if their taste hadn't made them so grotesque.

A small-eyed, shapeless little man, crushed by all the women, called out in a voice that sliced through the throng and set female flesh quivering: "As the giraffe said when he went into the cocktail bar, highballs on me, folks."

I struggled through them for another double whisky.

"The Soroptimists," said the barman without a smile; and I went to bed.

* * *

Burnley is beautiful for a passer-by, if you like steep streets and viaducts with steam trains swinging over the mills, and steel bridges across a street that are as likely to carry a canal as a railway, and tall chimneys, and hillsides coated with rooftops, and church steeples standing like cypresses in the main, and grubby little streams running down over the cobbles under old factory walls, and contrasts of every grey in a landscape where the only colour is in the green that sometimes touches the stone as though the moorland moisture had induced a slime, and in the bright advertisements for cigarettes and streaky bacon. But it's ugly when you think of living there, in one of those bleak rows of little houses that climb to the moors, the pavement slanting diagonally across the doorstep. They are tiny, those industrial revolution houses; the buses are twice the size.

But Burnely has turned its back on itself. The mills are still there, but they are no longer the whole point of the place. Many of them have closed down, and others have been turned into something else. No smoke comes from the tall chimneys, roofs have collapsed and blackened windows have been broken, as though the cotton girls, before quitting, had hurled their clogs at them, pane by pane. The scum in the canals that run high along the hillsides is unruffled by barges, and though the shaft wheel of the coal-mine in the middle of the town still turns, it turns without the old significance and without the old drama. Burnley was never a coal town, and now it is no longer even a cotton town. The modern factories round the edge—bungalows beside the tall old buildings, with neither the stature nor the style—making motor tyres and electric cookers, are more prosperous than the remaining cotton mills; the television aerials and giant floodlights above the football stadium are more symbolic on the skyline than the mill chimneys; the stucco houses with stained glass front doors creeping out of town are more significant than the old cottages, now waiting to be demolished. Clearance is in the air. Things aren't what they used to be in Burnley; and Burnley is mighty glad they aren't.

The year 1913 was Burnley's glory, just as it was Lowestoft's glory; more cotton than ever before or since, and more herrings. Some people would say that 1913 was England's glory too, with more battleships and more colonies, more self-confidence and more symmetry. But Burnley, at any rate, prefers it as it is now:

more choice, more money, more muddle, more emptiness; less herrings, less cotton.

I went into the parish church, on a rock washed on three sides by a dirty river down from the moors. Inside, an oak cabinet had just been dedicated in memory of the men who were killed in a coal-mine disaster two years ago; but they might as well have been drowned in the *Titanic* fifty years ago, for all the relevance such things had to modern Burnley. Besides, it was Grand National day, the ground was soft at Aintree, and in the pubs the talk was all of stayers and mudlarks and ankle-deepers.

I walked through a public park, where rooks were flying above the bare trees carrying sticks for their nests, back to the hotel for lunch. In the dining-room recorded music dribbled like the lamp-shades from the ceiling and each plate was laid with a card read-ing, "May digestion wait upon appetite"; and though the dust was settling on the gâteau trolley, the businessmen had telephones brought to their tables, as they do in films, and the food was as momentous as the conversation.

"Now I'm going to be very, very naughty. I'm going to talk shop."

"Let me put it this way: I can push it like hell."

"Why, in Minneapolis we have our problems too."

"Let's say a letter of credit dated April first."

"I think we could put in a pre-heater."

"I tell you, it takes me weeks to get accustomed to your English coffee."

"You know why?"

"Roasting."

"Water."

"All it is, is a tweezer-welding; that's all it is."

It rained all afternoon but I had to get out, and I followed a notice in the main street pointing to the Dog Show. It led me past the market, up round the station, along the road to Nelson, back round the church, and into the main street again. It must have been one of those elaborate Lancashire jokes, like the man in the car who had a skull lying on the back seat, or the star-studded neon sign 'Come dancing', which in Burnley means 'Come and play bingo'.

I found a policeman standing hunched like a hooded crow in

the rain and asked him where I could get a bus to take me up on to the moors.

"Down there, you see that big black building? I shouldn't say that really; it's a church. Then you see that nice white building? That's police station. Bus station's the other side."

The bus took me up past cemeteries and rubbish tips, past a Salvation Army citadel, far out of the rain and up among the waterworks. I walked all afternoon along a switchback road, through windy, misty, wuthering country, where soggy sheep nibbled at the grass, and the dregs of the winter's snow, grubby and hard-packed, still lay piled against the stone walls. In the hamlets children in wellingtons and sou'westers splashed through the puddles, and gas-lamps shone yellow and forgotten in the afternoon.

That Saturday night I had a beer in a couple of pubs, hurried past a fish and chips shop, reached a cinema half an hour after the film had begun, was refused admission to the bingo hall because I wasn't a member, ate a terrible meal in a Chinese restaurant, and ended up in a club. I paid half-a-crown to go in as a visitor, and signed a ticket to say I wouldn't buy myself a drink. To test it I bought a beer at each of the three bars; the only difficulty was that at two of them I was given short change.

In a huge room that might once have been the town hall, with the Victorian decoration obliterated by contemporary additions, a comedian pattered away into a microphone and a huge audience amused itself with beer. A big woman with a tight skirt caught round her thighs and a spotlight on her bosom came down off the stage and sang her way unconvincingly among the tables; and then a family of Hungarian acrobats tumbled and juggled for our delight, until they ran out of tricks and whistled up a family of poodles to take over. The place only livened up when the Cyclones took the stage and the teen-agers of Burnley took the floor.

I saw a door marked Tudor Bar, and with thoughts of the one at Skegness and a vague idea that I might end up where I had started, I went in. But it was better than anything at Butlin's; under the mock beams and orange lanterns, the young and old and rich and poor of Burnley were gambling.

For half an hour I watched roulette. Croupiers in dinner jackets called out the old French words in new Lancashire translations, while the ball rattled round the beautiful, terrible wheel. There were young men throwing coins down on to the green baize, and girls watching with admiration, and a wizened little man with a bundle of notes who consulted a card and staked ten pounds and doubled his money and staked the lot and lost it, and looked as though he was prepared to go on like that all night; there were gamblers with systems, betting on a plan, and gamblers tossing down ten-shilling notes haphazardly, and gamblers carefully laying half-crowns across a line between two numbers; there were timid gamblers, and confident ones with an air of knowing every casino in Europe, and cautious ones and reckless ones and would-be ones hovering at a distance with glasses of beer, fascinated by the danger or appalled by the stupidity. And all the time the wheel spun and the little ball rattled.

I knew I was going to bet, just as I knew I was going to win. I made a pact—with fate, perhaps, or with the little ball, or with myself. It was a certainty; there was no danger at all; but still I was terrified. I watched the ball hypnotically, with utter confidence, and with horror. It was so simple and inevitable that it wasn't even exciting; and yet I was sweating with fear. It must have been like suicide; I had made a decision, and I knew what would happen. I had a five-pound note. I would double it, just once; and then I would go away.

If the ball fell into a number between one and eighteen it was *manque*; between nineteen and thirty-six it was *passe*. Discounting the unlikely possibility of it falling into zero, the chances were exactly even that it would be *manque* or *passe*. I decided to bet on *passe*.

I waited and watched; and then, three times running, it fell into *manque*. As the croupier dropped the ball into the wheel again I pulled out my fiver, leaned forward and put it on *passe*.

Immediately I was seized with shame, worse even than my terror. I knew that the law of averages doesn't work for single cases, and the chances of it being *passe* were no greater for following a run of three *manques* in succession; the chances were still exactly even, and I was a fool to suppose that it couldn't be a fourth *manque*. And so I went on sweating. But I also knew that I was going to win; I had made a pact.

I didn't watch the ball, though I could hear it rattling on the wheel. I looked nowhere—at the ceiling, at the walls, at the faces, seeing nothing. I tried to appear nonchalant, but I knew that, with shame and terror and confidence all on my face, I hadn't a hope.

Then suddenly the rattling stopped; the ball had fallen in a number. Even before the croupier called it out, I knew what it was. A high number. *Passe*. The croupier gave me my fiver back and counted out five pound notes. I didn't smile. I didn't say anything. I didn't look at anything. I still couldn't see, though I longed to know if anyone was looking at me as I walked out.